The Life of Yeshua

Peter Marks

Onwards and Upwards Publishers,
Berkeley House,
11 Nightingale Crescent,
West Horsley,
Surrey,
KT24 6PD,
UK.

www.onwardsandupwards.org

copyright © Peter Marks 2016

The right of Peter Marks to be identified as the author of this work has been asserted by the author in accordance with the Copyright, Designs and Patents Act 1988.

All rights reserved.

No part of this publication may be reproduced or transmitted in any form or by any means, electronic or mechanical, including photocopy, recording or any information storage and retrieval system, without permission in writing from the author or publisher.

Scripture quotations are taken from the New King James Version®. Copyright © 1982 by Thomas Nelson. Used by permission. All rights reserved.

ISBN: 978-1-910197-99-8

Cover design: L M Graphic Design

Printed in the UK

Peter Marks

Author's Note

The book you hold in your hands is a work of fiction based upon the God-inspired true history of the Gospels. These pages tell of One whose story will thrill your heart as you open your Bible.

The Life of Yeshua

Chapter One

Facing each other across the shingle, the brothers grasped the great net in their fists. One violent shake and a myriad clear droplets arched into a rainbow above their heads, together with a hail of gravel, twigs and fragments of green weed dredged up from the bed of the Galilean Lake. Lake Galilee, the jewel of Israel! Skimmed by summer swallows, home to families of fussy moorhens busy among the water lilies. Solemn, beady-eyed herons gliding soundlessly overhead or frozen into watchfulness among the pebbly shallows.

The east and westward shores of the lake were seldom visible to the barefoot children from the villages around the northern town of Capernaum, especially on misty mornings or in sudden blinding rain – squalls which seemed to come from nowhere, capable of swamping the sturdiest craft and upending it to vanish beneath the dark waves.

A group of ragged children appeared now, racing over the shingle to swing upon the low willows overhanging the shallow water, dabbling their toes in the reflection of the trees.

Flinging the end of the dripping net over the pole, Andrew watched them wistfully. "They're about early" he said.

"Day off from school," Simon grunted, shaking drips from his face and busily picking grit and crustaceans from their limp net. He was still sore at heart, having given his all to their night's fishing with no reward. Their empty net held nothing with which they might fill their row of empty pots sitting open-mouthed near the ashes of last evening's fire. That was a fisherman's life! It often happened. The way of the elusive fish was still a mystery. No one Simon had ever met knew all the secrets of the art of fishing the lake, where men met and wrestled with the sea and all the creatures which lived within its deep waters. How deep was Lake Galilee? No one knew.

Surrounded by windswept hills, set in a grassy plain, the river poured and gushed down from the northern mountains in the season of melting snow, stirring and refreshing the deep. At the southern end of the lake, water flowed quietly down to the Salt Sea where it swirled and settled, finally evaporating into mist. Nothing lived in the Salt Sea, neither fish nor weeds, not a snail, lizard or spider. All was salt, not a trace of life.

By contrast the Sea of Galilee was alive – sparkling with fish leaping in the sunshine. Shoals, shooting through moving clear water like silver arrows. Clever fish, too. Surprise was the chief factor towards a good night's catch. Simon and Andrew knew that only too well. Quietly does it!

Farther down the beach James and John were shaking out their own net, having been out all night. After sharing supper the four had pushed their boats, without a splash, into the deep, heading for the mysterious gathering places of the shoals. Dusk had fallen, turning the hills a deeper blue. The two boats had glided across the calm water, their stiff sails aimed to catch the slightest breeze.

Simon, strong and bare-chested, quietly slipped over the side into the calm water. Leaning over, Andrew handed his brother the end of the net, which began to unroll as Simon swam out with strong strokes. As he turned back, the weighted net sank in an upright position and curved around. The fish came alive after dark to feed in great shoals. Sometimes a whole school of them might rush at once into the net, whose ends would then be drawn together – and the trap was closed. Most times, however, just a few strays would be caught and brought back to be sorted then packed in salt for the markets around the lakeside towns. Whatever the catch, the nets had always to be washed, carefully cleaned, then draped to dry on poles near the beached boats.

Dawn had seen the fishermen rowing back to the beach exhausted. It had been another fruitless night. Nothing had found its way into their nets, either good or bad. But the nets still had to be picked clean, washed and left to dry before the tired fishermen made their way home.

Simon and Andrew lived in Capernaum, just a short walk along the shore. Today they would be going home empty-handed.

People were coming. That was strange! The dew still stood on the few bushes which lined the dusty road. Most of the dawn traffic – a few carts, donkeys, early risers, who chose to go off to work in the cool of the day –

The Life of Yeshua

should have been going in the opposite direction. Quite a crowd was approaching. Some excited boys were running along the beach in order to keep up. At the head of the crowd, out-stepping them all, came a young, powerfully built man, whom Simon instantly recognised as Yeshua of Nazareth. Simon had met him once before, a meeting which had stirred Simon's deepest thoughts. Then life and work had swept them apart.

There seemed to be no end to the growing crowd; all kinds of people, many running to keep close to Yeshua. With a shock Simon realised that the Teacher was making straight for him. He felt, strangely, that his legs had lost their power of movement! The Teacher stood in front of him as the crowd gathered, pressing closely around. There was no preamble –

"I need to use your ship."

Simon gazed into Yeshua's face, spellbound by a regal authority, a pure kindness and depth of wisdom, combined with an irresistible urgency and determination which he had never imagined in any other human being. There was no time to consider further. Simon had to exert all his strength not to embrace this stranger, or fall at his feet. There was nothing Simon could or would have refused him. Springing up, the fisherman put his massive shoulder to the boat, pushing it backwards into the gently lapping water. The Teacher climbed in and sat down in the prow. Perfect stillness fell.

Yeshua began to teach the Kingdom of God in a strong, clear voice. His unmistakeable tones could easily have carried to the foot of the surrounding hills.

Thoughts chased each other inside Simon's head – *Who is this?* Utter silence prevailed among that vast congregation stretched along the beach, a silence upon which the Master's clear tones painted pictures of the wonders of God's creation, man's responsibility, coming trials, and joys; choices which would affect their now and forever. Simon's eyes never left the Master's face. No man had ever spoken like this before. It was like listening to God's own voice speaking from Heaven as he had done in past centuries. Andrew, James and John seemed to be gazing at something indescribably beautiful. A baker, standing near John, had his eyes closed as if listening to the finest music, or a nightingale.

After long moments lost in time, the Master finished his teaching with a final word to all to turn away from the empty promises of the world and instead seek the Kingdom of God and his love. A great sigh rippled through the vast multitude. Gradually they began to drift away, expressions of wonder and deep concern on many faces.

Simon, confused, turned again to his net. Something caused him to look up. The Master was standing in the ship. He reached a hand to Simon.

"Launch your boat into the deep," he said. "Make your nets ready for a catch." His words were friendly, but imperative; it was a command.

Simon gazed at him open-mouthed. Andrew joined him. Did the Master know about fishing? Surely not! The water lapped Simon's sandalled feet. "Master," he said quickly, "we've been out all night – nothing's happening."

He raised his eyes and saw something in the Master's face between encouragement and authority and added, "But if you say so, we'll go."

With Yeshua still aboard, Andrew and his brother put their shoulders to the prow and heaved their boat into the sea, hurling a bundle of nets in as it turned. Each taking a long oar, the two propelled their craft some distance from the beach – a good place, but not the best. Expertly they unfolded the nets.

"One?" Simon muttered. Andrew nodded. One would do – to please the Master. They flung it wide, with less than their usual care. As it splashed and sank there came an unexpected impact, which tightened the ropes and caused the boat to shudder over thirty degrees, almost throwing Simon off his feet.

Beneath the reeling ship a great ball of shimmering silver buoyed up beside them. The single net was packed to bursting point with glittering silver fish – not a dark, inedible one among them. As the boat lurched, the rising net spilled into the stern of the vessel, now alive with waves of sliding, twisting fish. Only the Master remained calm. Frantically, Andrew waved to John and James, who had pushed out at the same time. Side by side the boats heaved in the water, fish still pouring into both vessels, until they barely stayed afloat. Nothing like this had ever been known in all the history of Israel.

Gasping, Simon turned to face the Master, standing on a cross-thwart, holding the mast – and suddenly Simon knew. He, the Master himself, was responsible for this. Simon was overwhelmed. He knew himself to be standing in the very presence of the Lord of all creation, the Son of God, the sovereign King of the universe. Simon, knee-deep in the purest, finest catch he could ever have imagined, suddenly became aware of his own unworthiness. As the boat ploughed along, he knelt down before the Lord Yeshua.

"Go away from me, Lord," he pleaded, "I'm nothing but a sinful man." Simon felt a touch. The Lord was smiling.

"Don't be afraid," he said. "From now on your 'catch' will be men."

It was an invitation which Simon could not refuse. He was left wondering what would have happened had he fully obeyed the Master and let down all his nets, instead of just one.

Chapter Two

Fancy bringing a camel through a narrow alley like this! Still, it was a shortcut – the notice said so, and a toll had to be paid to the Romans on all goods carried through. Levi stood up in his alcove as the great sandy-coloured animal stumbled and snorted, turning a scornful gaze upon the tax-gatherer. The camel driver uttered one sharp word and the animal stood still.

Beneath a faded rug thrown across its back, Levi noticed several bulging saddlebags. With a nod to the driver he threw up the rug and began rummaging in the bags. He found leather-craft goods, barrels of dates – and then his practised fingers discovered something else – a small, lumpy bag. Taking it to the light, Levi found several glittering stones – pure, uncut emeralds – and two shiny pearls. No wonder the unknown merchant was trying to get these to his ship with all haste. Levi drew a breath. This was going to be expensive. Making a calculation, he rapped a figure to the little turbaned driver, who, without hesitation, drew a purse from his belt and placed six silver coins on the table.

The tall, sandy shape plodded out of the alley, leaving the tax-gatherer staring at the six shining coins. Five would have done. Why should Rome have them all? Levi placed a finger over one coin. It would never be missed. Other rich merchants would gladly pay seven for a haul like that. Two for the tax-collector! No, having won the battle, Levi opened his official bag and angrily swept the coins inside. What kind of a fool was he?

People called Levi a traitor because he was a tax-gatherer for the hated Roman occupation. Six days of the week he sat at a table at the end of a narrow alley. The alley was a convenient shortcut between two main roads and anyone, rich man or peasant, bearing goods had to pay to enter or leave, according to what they carried. The more valuable the cargo, the more coins one needed to hand over. Sometimes a farmer with a bag of grain would be asked for more than the rate, because the tax-collector knew him as someone a partner held a grudge against.

Levi hated the work, but was clever at figures and needed a job. His only friends were the other tax-gatherers, who cheated and winked at people who gave them a little extra for 'concessions'. Many collectors kept two bags beneath their tables – one for the Emperor, the other for themselves. Everyone hated them. Even the Romans despised the 'traitors', and pushed the collectors aside when they came to collect the heavy bag at the end of the day.

Apart from the camel, there were few customers today. Yesterday had been market-day, when a Roman guard had stood near Levi's table for most of the time – but with a little care even these could be bribed.

Levi looked up as a Syrian wine-seller guided his laden donkey through the gap. He gave Levi a sly wink as he passed, but no coin. Levi knew that a large skin of

The Life of Yeshua

wine often found its way into the hands of the tax-collectors' fraternity, who regularly met in Levi's house.

On days like this Levi realised just how lonely he was. Children whispered behind him and shrank away. Women stopped talking together and hid their faces. People of his kind were looked upon as no better than thieves or robbers.

A farmer, carrying a small sack, hurried past and rolled a tiny coin across the table. Levi opened his mouth to wish the farmer 'Good day!' but he was gone. Levi sighed and counted his dish of small change once more and marked his clay tablet. A sudden wave of loneliness and misery overcame him. Oh, if only he could begin his life all over again!

The family of Levi, third son of their ancestor Jacob, had been famous in ancient Israel for living close to God. *Now look at me,* Levi thought. How he longed for a whole new beginning – even a new name – and to go once again to the synagogue to meet some real friends.

A donkey-cart plodded past on the main road. A small group of men waited for it to pass before crossing, heading for Levi's alley. They carried no bags, so could pass through without paying. But they were *not* passing through. Three of them stood back while their leader's shadow fell across Levi's table. He suddenly realised who his visitor was.

All the stories Levi had heard about Yeshua of Nazareth, all his gentleness with children and those who loved God, his strong warnings to those who ignored God and followed their own religion, all his wonderful words of life and hope flooded into Levi's mind. People were asking important questions about him. Now here he was in person!

Suddenly, all shyness, guilt and loneliness fell away from Levi. He looked up full into the Master's face and saw there the invitation and hope. Deep within his heart, Levi knew he was looking into the kingly face of God's Promised One, the Hope of Israel and of the whole world.

The Master's eyes shone. "Follow Me," he said.

Levi obeyed without one backward glance. His new life had begun.

Chapter Three

Four panting men stumbled along the rough path, each grasping one corner of a groaning bundle. There was no time to spare. Rumour had it that the Master had returned to Capernaum. Crowds were already gathering around Simon's house where he stayed, hoping for a glimpse of this one, whose words brought a breath of Heaven, and whose deeds proved that he was a man sent from God. A cry went up from the crowd – the rumour was true!

The Master came out and began moving quietly among the people, speaking to the blind, lifting the faces of the deaf to his, even restoring limbs where there were none, to the wonder and praise of their families. Wherever he moved, people leaped and danced, hugged each other and sang songs of praise to Israel's God. It was time now for teaching.

The sea of anxious faces surged forward attempting to follow the Master through the house door, into the wide room beyond, which was already packed. At the back of the room sat a group of oily-bearded, richly robed priests and Pharisees – no friends of the Master; they were here with one purpose – to catch Yeshua in his words and arrest him as a breaker of the Jewish law, much of it their own invention. No crowds ever followed them! Their jealousy of Yeshua had turned to hate.

Carefully stepping over legs and bodies, the Master found a place to sit and began to teach. Outside, the people had settled down to wait, content to know that their Lord was nearby and to gossip that whispered question – *Who is he? Could he even be God's Promised One – the Son of David?*

On the farthest edge of that quiet crowd the four weary friends paused. The bundle rolled up between them stirred and thrust out two arms. His helpless legs were as stiff as branches. The friends covered their cousin's useless limbs as best they could and explained the situation to him, for his mind was clear and unaffected by his ailment. The sufferer had been helpless since childhood, but blessed with a cheerful family of brothers and cousins, who cared for his every need. They were also a family watching and waiting for the coming of God's own son, promised by all Israel's prophets.

Each Sabbath, the family would attend the synagogue or travel up to the Temple for the seven annual festivals in Jerusalem, leaving their brother behind. At such times, placed in the shade by his sisters, he would pray and plead with God to forgive his sins so that he could be added to the number of Israel's true sons – because in those days the priests would turn away from the Temple all who were disabled.

The house where Yeshua taught seemed so far away. It was obvious they would never get to the front door – but get to Yeshua they must.

"Quick!" said one, suddenly. "Round to the back!"

Their cousin was heavy, they were nearly spent; but nothing could foil their determination to bring their needy friend to the Master. They made their stumbling way around the edge of the sprawling mass of people, knowing what they had to do. The blank wall at the back had a stone stairway built into it – but no handrail. This would be no easy task.

The tallest brother leaped up the bottom steps and grasped the patient's shoulders. His simple bed was already falling apart into loose strands. With help from below they lifted him step by step until, at last, their cousin and his ragged bed rested upon the low rooftop among rows of drying onions. Now for the real adventure! Voices arose from beneath them. The party on the flat roof were immediately above the room where the Master was teaching.

The roof was made of reeds and sticks plastered together. Layers of packed earth had been spread over the top where grass grew in the cool weather and made a shady outdoor room. With one accord, the four men began clearing away the earth from the roof with their bare hands. Cries of dismay came from below as a cloud of soil, dust and onions showered into the room. In the chaos, only the Master seemed undisturbed.

As daylight appeared above the heads of the people, the reason was seen for the bold intrusion. Four faces appeared, before a rugged bundle darkened the atmosphere and slowly descended, coming to rest in all its untidy folds right at the Master's feet. The man within the bundle struggled, his eyes fixed upon the Master, as he tried in vain to speak. But it was unnecessary. The Master was looking at him with all the warmth and compassion within him. Their eyes met, and the sufferer's heart suddenly leaped with hope and joy. The Temple priests looked taut and grim. What would happen now?

The Master paused, just long enough for every eye, every ear, to be once again turned towards him. His quiet voice filled the room.

"Fear not, my son. All your sins are forgiven".

A gasp went up from the back of the room. The faces of the bearded priests were masks of horror. What were they hearing? Who could forgive sins but God alone? This man was speaking blasphemy. Surely this was their opportunity!

Not a word was spoken, but the shocked silence told the whole story. The oily, horrified faces stared. The Master turned to confront them.

"Why do you imagine such things in your hearts?"

A stony silence greeted his question. Yeshua looked around at the ranks of faces, rich and poor, friendly and hostile, but all shocked at his words to the helpless man.

He continued, "Which is easier – to say to this man, 'Your sins are forgiven,' or to say, 'Arise – take up your bed and walk'?" The Master allowed a moment for this thought to sink in, then added, "But I will prove to you that the Son of Man" (the name he chose for himself) "does have authority upon earth to forgive sins…" Here Yeshua turned to the distorted, paralyzed sufferer and said, "Rise up – take your bed and go home!"

An amazed gasp travelled around the room. The whole party rose to their feet. On the floor before them a young, muscular man quietly moved his bed-rags aside and stood upon his feet. Standing before his Lord, his face radiant with unutterable joy, he raised his hand to Heaven in a victory salute. Then lowering his eyes, he picked up his bed and left.

Outside, shouts of triumph and praise to God echoed around the hills.

Simon stood alone in the empty room. A breeze touched his face from the ragged hole above his head. At his feet, just a patch of disturbed dust and plaster. The thought came again – *Who is this, radiating God's own love and power, bringing scripture alive, commanding the fish of the sea and now even forgiving sin in his own name?*

Chapter Four

One of the first things that Levi did after beginning to follow the Lord Yeshua was to arrange a great dinner for all his tax-gathering friends and anyone else who would like to come in. The families of the other disciples had gathered Levi into their fold, so warming his heart that his one desire was to tell the world how, at last, he had found real lasting treasure, and to share this treasure with all whom he met.

"Matthew!" Levi found that everyone was calling him by his new name. Perhaps the Lord himself had introduced him as Matthew, which meant 'gift of God'. He could hardly wait to go up to the Temple at Jerusalem and give thanks to God for his new life.

No one was busier than Matthew at the feast. Flushed and smiling, he hurried around the room and courtyard, directing the helpers, carrying steaming bowls and hot loaves to waiting groups. People of all kinds had come: cheats, tax-gatherers, all the worst characters; downright thieves, women who boldly followed the Romans for money, beggars and the despised. Matthew's one idea had been to introduce his new Master to as many folk as possible. He had even invited the priests and scribes. A few had responded but refused to come into the house.

When another of the Master's disciples stepped outside they stopped him. Andrew's heart sank when he saw their oiled beards and tasselled sleeves. They were the same Pharisees who had been in the house when the Lord Yeshua had healed the paralyzed man. Their spokesman's voice trembled as he pointed into the room, comfortably lit with banks of tiny oil lamps.

There came gentle laughter then a serious question, followed by silence as the Master's clear voice replied in his usual courteous but irrefutable way. A sigh was heard from around the room and a fresh clinking of cups. Such wisdom was here, such understanding of the scriptures. It was nowhere else to be found. Yeshua's very words healed broken lives and yet honoured God.

A smelly beggar staggered out of the door and vanished into the night.

The Pharisee shuddered and fell back as if afraid of something poisonous. He then repeated his question, pointing through the open doorway at the Master as he sat among the ragged poor and the rough market women. "How can he, if he is a prophet, sit among such people, even eating and drinking with them?" To share food and drink with someone was to welcome them into one's family – a great honour. Here was this Yeshua of Nazareth taking food with all the scum of society! Andrew failed to put his reply into words. It was as if he and the Pharisee were standing on either side of a deep ravine with no bridge between them.

Suddenly, the Master himself was by his side addressing the Pharisees. "It is the sick who need the doctor, not the healthy." There was an unmistakeable edge of rebuke in his voice. "I have come to call sinners, not the righteous. Go and learn what this means – I will have mercy and not sacrifice!"

The Pharisees started back in high indignation. Who would dare to address them in this fashion? They turned and walked away. The Lord's message was plain to Andrew. The street women and thieves were turning back to God – 'entering the Kingdom of Heaven' was how Yeshua described it. But the Pharisees would never enter until they gave up their pride and stopped despising ordinary people. And for the Pharisee this would be the hardest thing of all.

Chapter Five

Surely the hottest day of the year! So hot, that the few trees along the dusty, winding road out of Nazareth seemed to dance and shimmer in the haze. In the mornings crowds of people would visit this well – mainly women, with flimsy shawls around their heads and shoulders. Each carried a long cord attached to a heavy jar. The chatter would be happy family talk as the empty vessels descended, splashed and were drawn up brimful. There was often time for a whisper or two of local gossip, before the dripping jars were raised, in practised arms, to the tops of the women's heads. Today, however, the family talk was a little more serious.

The whole community in this part of Nazareth worked and lived closely together. Birth, deaths and weddings were the concern of the whole village, and today they discussed a problem. Mary's son had disappeared. He had not been seen in Nazareth for several weeks. "Always such a perfect help to his dear mother," one of the older women was saying, "especially since his father Joseph died. So obedient. Only had to raise her finger and he was there."

"Took up his father's trade," another woman added, drawing up her overflowing jar and resting it with others on the wide stone parapet.

"Supposed to be something peculiar about his birth, I believe," said another, hastily adding, "Not that I hold with all that angels business."

More women joined the group around the well, covering their heads against the sun, but anxious to join the discussion.

"What age would he be now?"

"About your age, I should think, dear," said another with a sly wink at the blushing thirty-year-old.

A dozen damp jars now rested on the wide parapet.

"Ah," said the first woman, "here comes Huldah. She'll know all the answers."

"She always does," someone finished, in an awed whisper.

The houses of the village stood huddled together like an arrangement of blinding white boxes against the fierce blue sky.

The dark, tottering figure of old Huldah made its slow, determined way up the dusty slope towards them, a large earthenware jar balanced awkwardly upon her bent back. Huldah was of great age and greater wisdom. Immediately, her neighbours involved her in their talk. What had happened to Mary's devoted son, Yeshua? Why had he suddenly left home and work; was it simply neglect? Where could he go with the Romans so watchful and their own religious leaders so ready to condemn anything out of the ordinary?

"What do you think, Huldah – has he gone to join his cousin John at the Jordan? Crowds of people are flocking to his baptism!"

The Life of Yeshua

"John's cry shakes the very hills," a young woman said. "He tells everyone – Jews, Romans, foreigners – they must give up all cheating and pride, and clear a pathway for God's Coming One."

"Yes," another put in, "and then be baptised in the river as a sign that they are now clean and watching for God's Kingdom to appear. But what about Mary's son? Where does he fit in?"

Every eye turned towards the old lady. Her brown, wrinkled face lit up in a smile, every trace of weariness vanishing in a moment.

Huldah had lived alone for many years. Long ago her father had been a leader of the synagogue where the people of the village would meet on the Sabbath day to hear the scriptures read and sing praises to the God of Israel. In the course of time her father, who was also a scribe, had given his only child five large scrolls of parchment, all written over with scriptures, and had taught her to read them.

"What do you think, Huldah?"

The elderly prophetess lifted her face to a sudden cooling breeze and raised her hand to the flawless blue sky. "The young prophet is safe," she said. "He is God's chosen Lamb, following his Heavenly Father's call. He will bring light and truth and the love of Heaven to Israel. They will hate him and try to extinguish that light, but eventually it will beam to the ends of the earth, to all the peoples of the world."

As Huldah's diminishing form faded into the haze, her thin dress wet from her unsteady burden, the others sat in silence. No more questions were needed. Everyone knew that Huldah lived close to God. She would know.

Chapter Six

Sabbath morning. A steady stream of people in their best clothes, if they had any, would soon be making their way to the synagogue in this poorer part of Nazareth.

Yacov was the leader of the synagogue. He and his family lived in the whitewashed house next door. His first job on the Sabbath was to unlock the back door, tidy the cushions on the best stone seats where the Pharisees sat in their finery, sprinkle some fresh mint on the floor, then unbar the main door to welcome the local worshippers. The rich were always greeted with much bowing and grimacing. The poor could squeeze in and stand where they might.

It was rumoured that the young carpenter Yeshua was coming back today. He would get a mixed reception if he did! If he really had a message from God, why did he not share it with the people of his own home town, who had helped to nurse him as a babe, seen him playing in the streets, and given him all manner of building work after his father, Joseph, had died? Surely, he owed his home town something! Why go all those miles away to Capernaum? The young teacher had been seen around those districts, apparently disturbing the peace and making enemies among synagogue leaders. But why go up to Galilee? After all, he was still known everywhere as Yeshua *of Nazareth*.

Sunlight began to stream through the apertures below the domed ceiling, shining into the gallery where the women and girls would sit or stand. A shaft of light touched the brass doors of the wall-cabinet behind the platform, known as the 'ark'. On Sabbath and festival days the treasured scrolls were taken out and unrolled for the reader of the day to use.

The morning wore on. The first villagers began to arrive: burly workmen, smooth-skinned officials, weary wives and mischievous-eyed schoolgirls.

The sunlight made a beautiful pathway through the open door right up to the ark upon the wall. The changing light from the door-fittings reflected bright patches around the room, which the younger children tried to catch in their hands. This kind of light only happened at certain times of the year. It seemed to lift everyone's spirits. The faces of the children were radiant. It must be a special day!

Long shadows mingled with the sunlight as a group of men and boys, each wearing a little skull-cap, filed in and greeted each other solemnly. Their mothers and sisters took the staircase on the left to the women's gallery.

Suddenly, quietly, he was there. He had returned. No fanfare, no white charger. Yeshua and two friends in his home synagogue on a Sabbath, just like old times – the homecoming carpenter, with his prayer shawl over his head like a peasant, ready to chant the praises of God.

The Life of Yeshua

The service began. The leader, Yacov, gave a few words of welcome, bowing obsequiously to the Pharisees. The cantor stood up and announced the first psalm by its title. People who knew that way of singing joined in. Others half-prayed the words which, of course, everyone knew by heart.

Then there came an exciting moment as Yacov stepped up to the ark. He opened the doors, revealing five large scrolls with wooden handles. Selecting one, he carefully unrolled it to a certain place and began to read from Deuteronomy in ancient Hebrew – which only the scholars could understand. The Pharisees sat nodding in agreement and stroking their oiled beards. Another Psalm came next, a more well-known one this time, and the children joined in.

After that, it was time to hear something from the old prophets of Israel. Today it would be Isaiah. Who would read? This was the moment when a craftsman or village elder would be allowed to come up and read – if he could – and even share a few thoughts from the Word of God. But at this point Yacov looked grim. Would this Yeshua come out to read? That was to be avoided. Other people in the congregation were looking over their shoulders, curious expressions on their faces. Yacov turned and faced the ark. Opening the twin doors he prayed quietly as he always did, "O Lord, let your Word bring life and joy to your people today. Amen."

There happened to be a visiting rabbi in the congregation that morning. A tall, gracious man, he had already led the prayers. Yacov would invite him to read from Isaiah and speak. Holding the treasured scroll in his arms, Yacov smiled and nodded an invitation to the white-robed rabbi, who raised his hand and politely declined. Yacov's face fell.

Quickly surveying the rows of faces, he saw Yeshua rise to his feet – and offer to come out and read. Yacov was left with no choice. "Come forward," he muttered.

A murmur of excitement moved the people in the gallery and below. But the moment Yeshua stepped on to the platform, silence fell. Every face turned towards him.

The young carpenter from the backstreet had stood there to read many times before, but had never spoken on the scriptures. His appearance had changed from those earlier days. No one could guess his age. His features were those of one who had spent many hours in the windswept hills and biting cold day and night. And yet, as he faced the congregation, he seemed so alive, and men shrank as he minutely surveyed the room.

The sun had risen higher now and was streaming through the apertures above them. The platform where the reader would sit was flooded with warm sunshine.

The silence was so intense that the ladies in the gallery could hear the stiff parchment being unrolled in Yeshua's hands. Reaching a certain passage he stopped, his eye still surveying every face before him, row upon row, all eager and waiting. Without lowering his eyes from their faces, he began to read words which had first been recorded seven hundred years before.

"The Spirit of the Lord is upon me. He has anointed me to preach good news to the poor, to heal the brokenhearted, to proclaim liberty to captives and restore the sight of the blind. To rescue those who are bowed down, and to tell out that the time has come when God will save his people." Rolling up the scroll, he returned it to a steward. Still closely observing the ranks of staring people, Yeshua announced, "This very day these scriptures are fulfilled in your hearing."

The visiting rabbi sat up. The words were clear and unmistakeable. This young man was treading the borders of blasphemy! Yet the authority of his manner could not be denied. The rabbi leaned forward, unable to take his eyes or ears away from the speaker, who addressed the mixed company calmly, yet with the air of a king addressing his subjects. No scribe or Pharisee had ever spoken like this before, or commanded such attention. His words were as refreshing as a pure river flowing through a dry and neglected channel, sweeping all the weed and rubbish before it, swirling its clear waters into every dark and diseased corner. His message was severe, yet filled with hope and joy.

The Kingdom of God is here!

Look again at the glorious Ten Commandments given to Israel. You are God's beloved people, his dearest treasure. How blessed you are! Turn again and seek after God. His Kingdom is here – now!

Delight was on every face. God was visiting his people. They almost broke out into spontaneous applause and songs of joy.

But all was not well. The Pharisees on the cushions frowned and leaned towards each other. Was this not

Joseph's son? Where did he get this way and this teaching from? Not from the college of the Pharisees! This man was drawing the people away from them, the guardians of God's inheritance. Something would have to be done. The carpenter must be trapped in his words and put away once and for all...

But the speaker's message had changed. You could not demand blessings from God as your right. Now the Pharisees sat up sharply.

"You will be asking why," Yeshua continued, "I do not do the same works here at home as are done at Capernaum. Truly, I tell you, no prophet is welcomed in his own country. Remember the famine in the days of Elijah? And yet, he was sent, not to a widow in Israel, but to a poor woman in Sidon. And in the time of Elisha many were sick in Israel, but none of them was made well – except Naaman the Syrian."

In one moment, the joy around the room subsided. Delight fell from their faces and changed to anger. Someone shouted – then there was uproar! Calmly Yeshua stepped from the platform and faced their grimaces and shaking fists. *How volatile are God's chosen nation!*

Yeshua strode to the door, his message complete. No one dared touch him for all the dust and anger hurled in his direction. By sheer weight of numbers he was propelled out of the town to the very edge of the rock-strewn hill upon which Nazareth was built. At this point he turned to survey the mob with regal sorrow, fixing them with his gaze. Some of the gathered ruffians, who had not even been in the meeting, had picked up stones. These could be heard to drop in the awesome silence. Without a word he walked towards them. They stood back and allowed him to pass, turning their heads to watch as he vanished into the distance.

Chapter Seven

Martha slipped out of bed, stepped into her sandals and stretched before the window. She was engaged to be married to a young potter in the next village, and today she and her mother would be opening the family chest to find material for her wedding dress. As she prepared breakfast, another thought kept coming into her mind. She had been in the women's gallery with her aunts and cousins. She had seen and heard what had taken place. She had heard the bellows of rage from the unruly mob and later learned how the Teacher had walked through them and out of the district. His absence from his home in Nazareth was keenly felt, so powerful was his personality. The strong, reserved young carpenter had gone forever. In his place stood an undeniable man of God, whose words and deeds swept everything before him. But where was he now?

Martha had some bakery to deliver to her aunt Elizabeth. Her way home led past the little pathway that led to Huldah's house. After greetings were done Martha told Huldah what had taken place at the synagogue and afterwards.

"What do you think?" Martha pleaded. "Is Yeshua God's promised Messiah of Israel?"

They were sitting beneath the shade of a tree next to Huldah's house. The old prophetess laid down her mixing bowl and stood in the full morning sunshine looking up at the sky.

"The pathway of the Son of God is marked out for him by his heavenly Father," she said. "He will endure sorrow – but great joy is set before him." She raised her thin, floury hands to heaven, looked up into the sky and whispered, "Glory to his name!"

Chapter Eight

After Nazareth, the Master had again journeyed north, his strongest followers keeping up with him and staying close. They were not far from Capernaum now, the plain of Gennesaret. Around them were wide areas of soft green grass. A murmuring stream ran nearby.

It was late afternoon when three disciples standing on the ridge called out, "Master, look!" Then with cries of amazement, "They're still following!" Below them a dark mass of moving people – young and old – walked, plunged or struggled towards the place where they knew that Yeshua would be. A countless throng of men and families, entire village populations, moving with one aim in mind – to get close to Yeshua of Nazareth and be blessed by him. Asking no questions, simply knowing by instinct that here was a man – perhaps *the* man – bringing the love and presence of God into their world. They knew that one day the promised Messiah must come, and everyone who had heard John Baptist knew that he had pointed out Yeshua as the Lamb of God, even if they did not know what he meant.

The fringe of the multitude was arriving. Children ran towards Yeshua, almost swinging him around. Laughing, he lifted them in his arms. The mothers were running now and trying to thrust their toddlers forward, a

The Life of Yeshua

swarm of urchins all yelling with delight. This was too much. Some of the disciples stepped in and waved the mothers away.

"No, no! The Master mustn't be bothered with your babies..."

"Stop!" said the Master. At once everyone was listening. Even the children paused, open-mouthed.

"Let these little ones come to me. Do not stand in their path. All who enter the Kingdom of Heaven are like these." Taking them up in his arms, Yeshua blessed them. "And, I tell you most truly," he continued, "not one of you will enter the Kingdom of Heaven unless he comes like one of these little children."

John was listening carefully. The urchins had ran and tumbled over each other in delight to get to Yeshua, asking no questions, coming just as they were, all hungry and unwashed, but allowing nothing to stand in their way for sheer joy.

A word from an old prophet came to John as he listened –

> *Behold, the Lord God shall come.*
> *He will feed His flock like a shepherd.*
> *He will gather the lambs in his arms*
> *Holding them close to Himself*
> *And gently lead those with young...*[1]

---

[1] Isaiah chapter 40 verses 10-11

The Master was still teaching. "More than that," he continued to a stunned silence, "if anyone puts a stumbling block before any of these little ones who believes in me, or causes one of them to stray," and here he looked around at the whole company, "it would be better for that person to have a millstone tied to his neck and be dropped into the deepest part of the sea."

More and yet more people were arriving and swelling the multitude, pressing upon each other to hear the Master's words. Many of them clung to each other, almost exhausted. Some of the children were crying.

Philip was standing near the Master. "We ought to send them away to buy bread. Some of them haven't eaten for a couple of days." Philip could see a huge problem coming.

The Lord looked at him. "You give them something to eat," he said.

Philip was aghast. He ran his eye over the crowds still arriving and swelling their numbers. "Two hundred days' wages wouldn't buy bread enough," the apostle protested, "even to give every individual just a morsel."

"Here's a boy with five barley cakes and two small fish," another added, "but what good is that?"

"Get them to sit down in parties on the grass," the Master replied, accepting the boy's gift.

The message was passed along, and after some time the entire company were seated on the grass like so many tiny islands of people, receding far into the distance – all trusting, all waiting, all at their last ounce of strength – and not a crumb between them; but each one looking to

The Life of Yeshua

the Shepherd of Israel, who was about to prove that he was indeed the great Provider of their every need.

In the silence that prevailed over that mile of greensward, only the ripple of the cool, shallow stream could be heard. Standing at the head of that vast table, the Master looked up to Heaven and gave thanks to his heavenly Father for the tiny meal set before them. Lifting up his hands, he gave praise to God, Lord of all creation, who, by His love and power, produces food from the bare ground to feed and nourish all the creatures of the earth. Then taking a small barley slice in his hands, he carefully broke it, as if it were something infinitely precious.

Andrew held out his hands. As Yeshua, with reverential solemnity, placed the food in them, the apostle became aware that he was, indeed, handling holy things. God's daily gift to his creatures for their need and wellbeing, but also a reminder that all the gifts poured out to us each day come from God's almighty hand.

As the other apostles waited, their Lord began to break and share the cheap bread-cakes together with the fish. Each disciple received a fair handful to begin passing from hand to hand and group to group. This would take some time.

With amazement the apostles – and their willing junior couriers – returned again and again to the head of the table, and still Yeshua sat patiently breaking the same bread, the same fish and calling empty-handed helpers to the front.

All across the grassy plain, families were fed. They drank from the clear stream, and ate again, as fresh supplies came forward – always the same cheap, wholesome barley cakes, broken in halves around delicious salt fish.

A great while later, the Lord placed the last broken bread into a waiting apostle's hands. The younger couriers had disappeared, their work complete, their own meal set aside for them. Groups nearby were beginning to stand up and brush the crumbs from their children's clothes.

A steady stream of families had begun to make their way down the valley, casting many a backward glance. The apostles were standing in a silent group, gazing in awe at their beloved Master.

Philip spoke first. "Five thousand," he murmured, "and all from five slips of bread and two sardines."

But the Lord had not finished. Knowing that by now his own disciples were famished, he spoke to his twelve. "Take a basket each and bring back the unused food. Let nothing be wasted."

Obediently, they spread out and walked the wide plain. Already the birds were feeding on the crumbs. Here and there were collations left behind, which the apostles carefully placed into the basket they were carrying. All twelve were filled and carried back, heavy and smelling as sweet and fresh as newly baked loaves.

A question remained in their wondering minds as they carried the evidence in their arms. Each of them knew that had the whole world been sat down before them in families, the Lord would have fed them all from those same five loaves and two fish. They already knew that nothing was impossible with God. But was anything impossible to Yeshua of Nazareth?

Chapter Nine

The Master and his twelve sat down to a late lunch. No one spoke, except for a chorus of "Amen" as once again their Master gave thanks. It was an awesome experience – enjoying a very ordinary lunch together, yet knowing that the food they ate was as mysterious as Israel's manna from Heaven.

John's eyes roamed that vast and empty plain. His love for the Master deepened every day, but each day the mystery also deepened. He knew that God alone could do the things Yeshua did. Yeshua came from the carpenters' shop with the smell of resin on his clothes. But who was he in truth?

Their meal complete, the twelve arose preparing to leave. At once the Master held up his hand and peered into the distance where the hills met the greensward. Knots of men could be seen gathering, having been fed, and sending their families on before them. Gathering together at a bowshot's distance, the large company of men began moving in the direction of the Lord and his disciples.

Yeshua turned to his twelve. "Take ship and aim for the northern shore. I shall join you shortly."

Simon's face fell. *What a haul!* The wind was getting up too. *But trust the Master – he knows what he's doing.*

Simon frowned again. *Sail won't be much good. Wonder how many of them can row...*

The Lord turned and strode towards the company of advancing men. They were almost running. He could see their faces now. Not hostile, but grim and determined. Some way off they halted in a ragged line and raised their voices.

"Yeshua of Nazareth, Son of David – Messiah! Promised One of God! You are rightful King of Judah! You will supply our every need! We shall drive the Romans from our land – together! We come to take and crown you king!"

Down at the water's edge, the disciples turned in dismay as some of the words floated back to them. What should they do? Would the Master allow the rabble to anoint him king? Surely never! Shading their eyes, they saw him halt before them and gesture as he addressed them. The whole mob seemed to have become immobile.

"Come," said James, drawing their attention to the task in hand, "lend your muscle to the launch."

The boat slid into the surf. The twelve clambered aboard, some needing a hand from the regular seafarers. A gust of rising wind hit their faces.

"What about the Master?" came a voice. But no one replied.

Back on land, cowed by the Lord's rebuke, the men drifted toward the town. Satisfied, the Lord swiftly took an upward path and was soon among the high rocks, skilfully using fingers and feet to climb towards a remote place on the mountain known only to himself. Fitful clouds began to race above him, driven from the north by treacherous gusts.

Turning again, the Lord could just make out the ship, tiny at that distance, battling with the sea in the rising wind. With his cloak thrown over his head the Lord turned to his Heavenly Father in prayer.

Darkness crept across the face of the Sea of Galilee. Twelve was a heavy load for this size of fishing craft. The rowers groaned together. They were almost spent. A light mist swirled around the ship. Familiar landmarks were no longer visible. The fishermen knew only that they must face into the wind and row. Everyone took a turn with the oars, but only the four experienced fisherman could make any headway. Eventually even *they* had to rest while fresh rowers held the oars. Simon alone of the party was game to continue. He stood by the mast and peered across the restless water, calm for a moment – a mass of crashing waves the next.

Andrew stepped up beside his brother, his hands red and sore. "Did he not say he'd chosen us to be with him and learn of him? And here we are, on a night we would never choose to put to sea, with no idea what to expect or where we shall finish up."

The boat creaked, rising and falling with the waves, as if breathing. Simon stared into the mist. "He often says he must work while it is day. Night comes when no-one can work."

"What does he mean?" Andrew asked.

"His time is short," Simon replied. "I dare not imagine what he means, but it's our part to trust where we don't understand."

It was James who saw it first – a dark shape on the edge of the mist, moving – no – wait... It could not be... A *human* figure – not swimming, but briskly walking, striding out across the surface of the sea.

James cried out. "It's a phantom! We're lost!"

The tall figure strode on, looking most un-phantom-like, as the storm tore at its clothes, blowing its cloak in every direction. James' frantic cry from the prow echoed all around the deck and soon all twelve disciples were howling in wonder and anguish at this very real man striding powerfully across the sea, ignoring the storm, which swirled ineffectively around him.

Suddenly, the figure paused, standing like a lighthouse in the midst of a turbulent sea. A familiar, powerful, unmistakeable, beloved, rejoicing voice lifted their hearts.

"It is I. Do not be afraid!"

In an amazed stillness in which no one breathed or moved and in which every eye was wide, half-unwillingly witness to this final answer to their questions, the windblown figure, their dear Master in very truth, walked over the surf towards the ship. One moment more and he had stepped lightly on board, dry shod.

The entire ship's company stood before Yeshua in wonder and praise. Then as one man in the lifting, wave-lapped ship, they knelt and murmured their homage.

"Indeed, Yeshua, you are the Son of the Living God, Messiah of Israel!"

The Life of Yeshua

Chapter Ten

The following day, the sea was calm and bright. People began to gather around the shore near the place where Yeshua had fed the thousands, searching for him whom they knew had not left in the ship with the disciples. Where could he be? Some of the younger element took boats and set sail in the direction the disciples had taken – including some of those who had been fed, and not a few of these who would have made him king.

Arriving at the opposite shore, they quickly found the twelve. They would soon find out what had become of the Teacher. To their surprise, there he was, standing among them. Instantly, the crowd surrounded him and began boldly questioning him. "Master – how did you get here? When did you arrive?"

Yeshua looked around at their amazed faces, seeing no sign of heart-hunger for God, just a desire for free supplies of food. Disappointment filled his heart. He longed for them, as children, to give them his all, but their wants were no greater than those of animals.

"I tell you most truly," he said to them, "you come seeking me, not because you understand the signs, but because of the free meal which you ate. Take my words to heart and seek not for the bread that perishes, but for the everlasting bread which only the Son of Man can provide."

"Lord," said one quiet voice in the crowd, "please give us that bread from now on."

Yeshua, the Master, turned to look in the direction of the voice. "I, myself, am that Bread of Life. The one who comes to me shall never hunger, and he who believes in me shall never thirst." He raised his eyes to the restless crowd. "The Bread of God is he who comes from Heaven to give Life to the world. You have seen me – yet you still refuse to believe! Yet even now, he who does come to me will never be turned away. Most positively I tell you – everyone who believes in me has everlasting Life."

Time was running out. The Master strode on. Weary disciples followed. There was very little conversation now. Whatever town or village they came to, the Master always made for the synagogue. That was where the people of Israel gathered to seek after God. The Pharisees were always there in their elevated seats near the platform from where they might keep a wary eye on the congregation.

In the early days of Israel's history, God had made the Sabbath a special day of rest. Not satisfied with that, the Pharisees – highly religious men, who could read and write the ancient languages – added hundreds of rules of their own. So that on the Sabbath (our Saturday), no family was allowed to light a fire, cook or go to the well and carry water. No work of any kind was allowed according to the proud Pharisees. And no one, especially the poor, dare argue!

The Life of Yeshua

Simon had never been in this synagogue before, many miles from his home and work. It was cool after the heat and dust of the road and smelled refreshingly of washed stone and mint. The scribes were there, waiting and watching. They had heard that Yeshua of Nazareth was in the district and that he spelled trouble.

The murmur of voices as people settled down suddenly changed to an excited whispering. The Pharisees turned to each other and frowned. The congregation grew tense, sensing that a battle was about to begin. But the question remained, which party was on the side of God? Yeshua of Nazareth or the unrelenting Pharisees?

Even before the synagogue leader had taken his place, Yeshua quietly walked to the front and surveyed the assembly, looking for a certain man. That man's expectations grew with every moment, his face alive with joy and hope. He was unseen by those around him but already forming a bond between himself and the Teacher, whom he had never met but had often seen in his dreams. This was his day, and when Yeshua, in the sudden silence, said, "Come out to me!" he knew that the Lord's words were for him alone.

The man with the withered arm hidden beneath his tunic leaped up. Struggling to the front, he stood between Yeshua and the seated Pharisees and scribes, his whole being quivering with expectation. Yeshua stood apart from him and lifted his voice to the whole assembly.

"Which is best on the Sabbath day – to do good or bad, to save life or to kill?"

Not one person moved. He might have been addressing a congregation of statues. Only their eyes shifted, from the Master to the shocked and furious Pharisees. The Master looked around at them, anger flashing from his eyes at the hardness of their hearts.

Turning to the trembling man, Yeshua gave him a command, which he had never been able to obey: "Stretch out your arm!"

With a cry of triumph, the man drew from his tunic his restored arm – clean, healthy and powerful as the other. His praises to God echoed around the stunned assembly.

Later that day, a procession of grim-faced Pharisees made their way to the palace of Herod. Together they would lay a plan for the final destruction of this audacious menace to their authority – this Yeshua. Yet the common people knew that God had been with him that day and not with the Pharisees.

Chapter Eleven

Home at last – Capernaum! Perhaps some peace and quiet! Simon's house, with the wide courtyard, had been 'home' to the twelve for over two years now, since they had begun to follow their Master; although most of their time had been spent in traversing the rugged, often dangerous, plains of Judah and Israel. Camping, sleeping, watching, praying – always a few strides behind their Master, who never faltered, never complained, but led them as a General before his army, as they entered town and village, ever moving onwards.

Hundreds were healed. Multitudes heard God's word of the Kingdom. Congregations and families throughout the land were divided. Most loved him. Some – the most powerful – hated him. But none could ignore him. People the length and breadth of the land either knew him or knew of him, and his name was spreading like a great forest fire, together with the question, *who can this be, this Yeshua of Nazareth?*

At Simon's home, the disciples enjoyed one day's rest. The Master himself was nowhere to be seen. Just after dawn next day, Matthew came into the room. Looking around at their sleeping forms, he clapped his hands. "Stir your stumps, lads, we're leaving – one more adventure – a holiday this time – and then Jerusalem!"

"Come away and rest for a while," the Master had said.

A holiday! *There must be a reason,* Andrew thought.

But today was the Sabbath, when no journey could begin. That meant one more visit to the synagogue – and into danger!

During the service, the Master was invited forward to speak after the scriptures had been read. As he began, a shadow fell across the doorway. A poor woman of no great age appeared. Bent almost double, she clung to the doorpost, wondering if she might be allowed to sit on the stairs which led to the women's gallery. After one glance the congregation ignored her. She was well known. The Pharisees stared disdainfully at her bent form. *Late again!* They disapproved of latecomers.

Yeshua paused in his teaching. Stepping from the platform, he called the woman to come to him. Every eye followed her painful progress from the doorway to his feet, agony in every step.

"Woman," said Yeshua, in deeply compassionate tones, touching her head with both his hands, "you are released from your torment."

A gasp and cries of surprise all around the room! Immediately, she stood tall, stretching her arms to Heaven, singing praises to God in a shrill voice. But her shining eyes never left the face of Yeshua.

Someone cried out, "Amen!" to her song. Willing hands escorted her upstairs.

A moment's silence... The assembly shifted uneasily. The tight-lipped synagogue leader strode on to the platform vacated by the Master and began to lecture the congregation. His voice shook with indignation. "There are six days in the week when men should work. Bring your sick on those days, not on the Sabbath!" Every eye and ear turned towards Yeshua of Nazareth.

"Hypocrite!" The word stung like a whiplash. "Does not each one of you loose his ass or his ox every Sabbath and lead him to water?"

Up in the gallery each woman's hand sought the hand of her neighbour.

"And ought not this woman, your own sister in Abraham, bound by Satan these eighteen years – should she not be loosed from bondage this Sabbath day?"

God had indeed turned their Sabbath into a jubilee of rejoicing. The faces of Yeshua's enemies were covered in shame. The reunited families poured out of the synagogue hugging each other and praising the Lord God of Israel for Yeshua their Champion.

Dawn broke the following day. Simon leaned against the doorpost. Even he, the strongest, was weary. They would be leaving soon. His mind was a confusion of shrill voices, of thin ragged arms grabbing and waving – pressing, scrambling crowds – hundreds of appealing faces wherever the disciples were led, from town to village, market and synagogue.

Work always began at daybreak wherever they stayed. The disciples would say, "Lord, they're all out there waiting – endless crowds."

The Master would reply, "Now it is time to move on and teach in other places. That is the reason why I was sent."

His answer left Simon wondering – *If the Master is God's Promised One, then of course he must awaken the whole of Israel to himself, bringing God's Word to as many as will listen.*

Thomas had been struggling with the problem since before sunrise. He counted the Master as the best friend he'd ever had; but as he wrapped slices of new bread in a clean cloth ready to pack, he knew that he would follow the Master to the end, whatever that end should be. A murmur of voices arose around him, as the other disciples tucked in the flaps of their carrying bags, preparing to leave while it was still cool.

Simon looked around him. His wife and her mother would normally be preparing the day's bread at this time, but here they were, bustling around helping the clumsier disciples to fix their simple bundles for the journey north. *In an hour's time this house will feel so empty,* Simon thought. Everyone else was too busy for conversation.

The Master? He alone seemed to gain fresh strength each morning, while his disciples lay exhausted where they had fallen the night before. Yeshua would rest for a time then vanish into the cool night to commune with his Heavenly Father, afterwards returning with fresh strength for another day of clamouring crowds, battles with the enemy and witnessing to the truth of who he was. He came in now, wet from the dew, his dear face lined and solemn.

The activity ceased. Some bowed their heads. John stared at him anxiously.

The Master spoke. "You must prepare for a longer journey today. Sometimes it will be marshy underfoot, but later it will be cooler and pleasant. Follow me closely."

Simon noticed that, uniquely in the party, the Master carried no bag. Judas clutched a small red drawbag beside his rucksack, the Master having delegated him as party treasurer – *a strange choice,* some thought.

The Master was already striding away into the distance. Quickly the others gathered their belongings together and said their farewells.

The Master had a way of finding old paths and shortcuts. The disciples followed him at some distance, a long, straggling line across the wilderness, before coming to a well-trodden road with tufts of coarse grass growing on each side.

"The road to Caesarea," Andrew muttered. "Surely we're not going up there – they're all foreigners – pagans. It's a Roman leisure centre!"

"It's a beautiful, peaceful place," his brother replied, "but the Master won't find many villages up there. It's all running water and shrines to Roman gods."

James caught them up. "All his wonderful works have been done among God's own people," he said. "His name is known from the Great Sea to the hills of Edom."

"Or nearly." Thomas appeared at his elbow, having paused to knock a stone from his shoe.

"Yes," James agreed, "even in Jerusalem. You know..." He glanced at the distant striding figure of the

Master as he reached a ridge. Glancing back at the Teacher's scattered flock, he continued, "I feel we haven't paid our last visit to God's Holy City."

Even John, the youngest, had given up trying to walk with Yeshua. He gazed at his retreating striding form. "That man is something greater than any of us can begin to imagine," he said.

"Something is driving him," Nathaniel added. "His time is short – but where is it all leading?

Thomas had caught up with the leaders. His face glowed with pride. "David's throne's been empty a good many years now, and the Master's just the man to fill it!"

John frowned as he walked on. Their ideas were off the track, he was certain. Something was missing! But perhaps the Master was about to provide an answer.

Some way ahead, the Master turned abruptly from the main road, aiming to cross a marshy area.

"Careful!" someone called. Poisonous snakes lived among the reeds. The disciples' line straggled out again into single file.

"How does he know all these old paths?" Judas muttered to himself.

To their right was a gently rising plain of green grass. In the distance an old shepherd tended a flock of long-eared, parti-coloured sheep. He stood still as they passed some way below him, the Master well ahead, the twelve strung out behind.

As if in recognition, he suddenly stood erect among his sheep, raised his crook and stood in an attitude of salute until they had passed from his sight. John's heart warmed. *Even he, in this remote place, knows that something is happening in God's Israel, and that our Master, Yeshua of Nazareth, is at the centre of it.*

The ground was steadily growing steeper. Distant mountains were coming into view through the blue haze. In several places tall rocks flanked the narrowing path. As they followed the Master through the poplar woods, grateful for the dappled shade – nothing like this grew in Judea! – they noticed that the Master had halted by an evergreen acacia bush. Pushing the foliage aside, he revealed a bubbling spring of clear water. With cries of joy the disciples knelt down, burying their faces in the cold pool before lying back exhausted. But there was little time for rest.

Their journey lengthened, now a full two days and nights. The clamour of town and people had been left far behind. After dark the Master would join them around the camp fire, share a meal with them and lead them in prayer. He would then melt into the shadows again unseen, but never far away, like a caring shepherd.

As he prepared himself for sleep, Simon constantly reviewed his thoughts. Was the Master leading his twelve away to a peaceful place of recuperation, or had he something greater in mind? Was he, after all, going to gather a great army in some remote place and make them its generals? That could surely never be. Had he not said that those who live by the sword shall die by the sword? Yeshua's weapons in his fight against evil were love, truth and invincible power over cruelty and pride. He had shown himself Lord, even over the terrifying powers of the sea. Simon turned on his elbow as a twig fell into the heart of the fading fire, blazing up for a moment. *Trust the Master in all things.* Simon's heart swelled with love and pride as he sleepily gazed at the recumbent forms of his sleeping companions. *Yeshua chose us – God knows why.*

What was wrong with Iscariot? Simon felt a sudden chill as he caught sight of the treasurer's wide awake face in the fading glow. Simon saw him glance suspiciously around and then creep to the luggage pile. Groping beneath a dark branch, he suddenly seemed satisfied. Simon heard the faint *click* of a fastened latch. Judas, with one more furtive glance around, returned to his place. *Strange fellow!* Yet the Master had chosen him too.

It was hilly country now, against a background of much higher mountains in a blue-grey haze, sometimes covered in thin cloud. The stony slopes were treacherous beneath their feet, but the air felt fresh and clean, with just the faintest odour of cut pines. The Master left the open path once more and headed for the only visible trees, a group of gnarled firs covered in strong smelling sap. A trail of sunken, moss-covered stones led to an arched entrance formed of two incredibly ancient pines entwined together. The disciples bunched together, hesitating.

"An old pagan shrine," Nathaniel murmured. "What does the Master want here?"

Ivy-covered stone seats, discoloured with age and cracked by centuries of harsh winds and glaring sun, had been arranged in a circle around a grimy headless statue holding a lyre – mute and futile, as all idols of worship must be.

Boldly the Master stepped forward and moved a rock. Another spring, more powerful and beautiful than the last, burst out. "The spring is God's gift for all thirsting travellers," he explained, "but touch nothing else – nor enter without me."

Chapter Twelve

It became necessary to get one proper night's rest. That meant breaking their journey and crossing part of the wilderness to the nearest town. They had stayed briefly at a hostel for travellers, but even there, some ninety miles from Jerusalem, curious crowds had gathered. Hastily they filled their water bottles and left early.

So unbearably hot! Thaddeus screwed up his eyes against the glare and made for the solitary tree ahead. Five minutes rest, a welcome drink and then on – across the plain, among the thistles and bare rocks.

John turned suddenly. Was that the harsh cry of a bird? They had left behind the borders of Sidon and Tyre, that thriving port, where few Jews lived except for a few rich merchants. Down the long, shallow slope behind them John could see a huddle of buildings. Beyond the houses, shimmering in the heat haze, he could see a pillar of smoke rising in the still air from the centre of a grove of evergreen trees. "Pagan Canaanites," he said to Thaddeus, at his elbow. From the hill the disciples now crossed, fires could be seen blazing from those groves on festival nights with the sound of unearthly chanting, the thump of drums and sometimes the most chilling of screams. The Jews avoided the Samaritans as foreigners, but at least they professed to believe in God. These people were descended from the savage Canaanites of old.

There was that cry again! No large bird wheeled above their heads, but scrambling up the slope towards them was a Canaanite woman, dirty and exhausted from her climb, frantically calling out to the Master.

"Yeshua – Son of David! Help me – please – oh!" Sliding on the scree, she almost fell again, but persisted in her cries. "Son of David – mercy!"

Anger arose in Thaddeus' throat. How dare she, a foreigner, enemy of God and Israel, call the Master Messiah? What was that to her? She was so evidently a Canaanite from Syro-Phoenicia, descended from those ancient, hostile tribes, who performed unspeakable acts as they worshipped idols of wood and stone.

The woman stretched to grasp the Master's feet, but he walked on. Her face, arms and neck were tattooed in red, but tears streamed down her face.

Some of the disciples caught up with him, horrified and embarrassed. "Lord, send her away!" they pleaded.

Without breaking his steady step, the Lord replied, "I am only sent to the lost sheep of Israel."

That was true. God's promises were to His chosen people first, then to the world in a coming day.

The woman let out a final agonised scream, and threw herself on Yeshua's feet. "My daughter is tormented by a devil day and night. Please – only you..." she whimpered into the hem of his cloak, her face a mask of supplication, bathed in desperate tears.

Yeshua looked closely at her. His voice was firm but gentle. "It is not good to throw the children's bread to the dogs."

His disciples were shocked beyond words. But the woman lifted her tear-wet face to his and tried to smile.

"True, Lord, but even the dogs are allowed to catch the crumbs that fall from the Master's table!"

A moment of heavenly understanding seemed to pass between them. Her faith had been tested and the woman had responded with the faith and wisdom which always brings answers to prayer.

"Go home in peace," Yeshua replied, "your daughter is well again."

Chapter Thirteen

Surely their journey would be over soon! None of the twelve had ever been so far north, near the source of the river Jordan. On every side were rock faces, gullies and pouring torrents. They were somewhere near Caesarea Philippi, but no one knew exactly where. Above them stood massive Mount Hermon, capped with snow, seemingly inaccessible. Below them a gorge of broken rocks tumbled down to a glittering stream.

The disciples looked at each other above the roar of the surrounding waterfalls. They had reached their limit. No other people or habitations were near. What would the Lord do now?

A step down below a shelf of rock led them to a quiet arbour where, at last, they could hear each other speak. It was dry and comfortable here. There were the black remains of a fire, even a pile of fuel.

Matthew laughed, "We could bed down in a place like this!"

The Master gave thanks before they shared their simple meal of bread, fish and fresh watercress. He waited until all had finished, then he looked up. Immediately, he had their full attention, every face alert and waiting. They had learned that Yeshua was Master in every sense of the word, yet it was a joyful captivity. Their hearts pounded with expectation. He would go on from glory to glory.

Nothing, no one, could stand in his way. *Yet we,* Matthew thought, *are chosen to be part of it all, for some great reason.*

The peace, the gentle sound of moving branches and falling water, added to the atmosphere of freedom and joy in that heavenly arbour. When fully assured of their attention, Yeshua spoke.

"Who do the people say that I am?"

His searching glance embraced them all. They were to consider everything they had seen and heard since their Master had gathered them, all the astounding works done at his word, all across Galilee and Judea.

Matthew was still recovering from that unforgettable moment when God had called and delivered him from his hated past life. True, it had been Yeshua's face and invitation which had released him that day; and yet Matthew, known as Levi in those distant days, knew it was the voice of God changing his life forever.

Matthew was also well qualified to answer the Master. He still moved among people of the world who knew him. Around the cheerful market stalls he had met a fruit seller who had once been an outcast leper. "Look at me, man," the seller said. "Yeshua touched me – me, a leper from my first footsteps. He's my hero – he's Jeremiah and Daniel rolled into one!" Everywhere in that Galilean market the chatter never ceased – how Elijah had returned, or even a new prophet sent from God.

Nathaniel had recollections too. His gaze strayed over the jutting rocks at the top of the cliff where a couple of trees leaned over into the valley, moving in the breeze like people waving palms to greet their King. He was thinking of those scores of grotesque creatures brought screaming and writhing to be laid at the Master's feet. So gentle with the childlike and meek, he would be exceptionally severe with these. The sufferers would collapse, make awful distortions of their features and bellow in unnatural voices.

"What do you want with us, Yeshua? Go away! We know who you are – you're the Holy One of God!"

With one word of command the Master would point at the frantic creature and say, "Silence! Come out – leave!"

With a scream the child, woman or man would thrash the dust for a moment, then lie still – and wake bewildered, as if from a bad dream.

Time after time, the question came into the minds of the disciples and the common people – even in Herod's palace. *Who is this, having power over the waves, over living creatures, over unknown enemy forces?* All the time fragments of prophetic scripture came to the mind of discerning watchers and listeners – verses of praise and wisdom, daily fulfilled before their very eyes.

Simon began to understand some kind of picture of the Lord's purpose. God had promised a Saviour and a King for Israel and for the world. People were asking, *when the Messiah comes, will he do more than this man? Can this be the Promised One of God?* Simon's picture became clearer. *Of course! If Yeshua really is the Son of God, then his words and his deeds must speak for themselves, living proof for those with eyes to see.*

The Master repeated his question clearly and quietly, "Who do the people say that I am?"

"Jeremiah," Matthew offered.

Heads nodded in agreement.

"Elijah," said Thaddeus, naming another powerful voice from Israel's past.

John Baptist and earlier prophets were named – all great men of Israel – undeniably sent by God to bring his message and do great works among his people. Now Yeshua had swept everything before him in his Heavenly Father's name, and the people had responded, giving him the highest possible honour – except one!

Again, the Lord's eyes searched their faces, "And you. Who do *you* say that I am?"

Yeshua's power was invincible. Far greater than any Messiah that John could imagine, or that the best scribes taught behind closed doors. Yet in all his teachings he spoke peace, harmony and obedience to God's Word, sharply diverting any suggestion of rebellion or defiance; yet Simon sensed an edge in his words to the Pharisees that should clearly warn them of a judgement to come.

Something like love had touched John deep in his heart. Perhaps in looking for a military leader the people and their teachers had missed something far better. Had not the Lord told them that those who live by the sword shall die by the sword? Had he not also reminded them all that God's thoughts are not like men's thoughts? John, as well as Simon, was growing into a deeper understanding of their beloved Master, Yeshua.

The Master was repeating this question too: "Who do you say that I am?"

Someone must speak for them all. John's heart was too full for words.

Suddenly, Simon was on his feet, his eye bright. "You are the Christ – Messiah – Son of the Living God"

"How blessed you are, Simon bar-Jona!" The words came like a trumpet call, in a voice they had never heard before, echoing from that cave-like place down into the valley. The roar of the water seemed to echo the joy and the triumph. "The words of men have not revealed this to you, but my Father in Heaven. And I say to you, you are 'Petros' (a stone). I will build my Church upon this Rock, and the gates of Hades shall not defeat it!"

A new name! Peter now! Simon was astounded. Whatever could the Master mean? Peter was so aware of his weakness and failures. Did his simple faith and joy in watching and walking with Yeshua wipe all that out and qualify him, a mere fisherman, to take authority over the Kingdom of God? There must be some explanation.

The Master was speaking again – shattering, unbearable statements this time, all about his "rejection", "capture" and "execution" by the governing Roman power. The disciples were horrified.

Now Simon Peter had been placed, it seemed, in a position of leadership. More confused than ever, he realised that he must speak. He blundered forward. "Master – this shall not be. Turn your mind from such things!"

In a moment of stillness, the look which the Lord turned upon Simon might have destroyed armies. Then the trumpet voice again. "Out of my road, Satan! You are an offence to me. Your ideas come from men – not from God!"

The earth had been pulled from beneath Peter's feet. His desolation was complete. The rebuke stung for several days. Simon Peter's daily bread became dry and tasteless.

They journeyed on through hilly regions, stumbling along rugged paths, past groups of scrawny brown sheep, which shied away as they approached. The Master began teaching the twelve that in following him they would find hardship – not a life beneath a canopy of rich provision safe from all harm, but a daily prospect of facing persecution for Yeshua's sake. Proclaiming Yeshua as the world's Saviour would bring great opposition, especially from their rulers. They must share their Lord's burden, often relying simply upon God for the next food or night's rest.

Simon Peter began to realise that the Lord's first words to him reflected the joy of Heaven each time someone publicly expresses his faith in God's own Son, and that faith in Yeshua is the Rock upon which he will build his Church – not upon one weak believer! Also, that the Master's rebuke was God's warning to anyone who might try to turn God's Lamb from his final goal. Jerusalem held the key to that mystery.

Early next morning, the Master touched James, Peter and John, telling them to make provision for following

The Life of Yeshua

him up the mountain. Peter's heart gave a leap. He had been forgiven.

After a scramble over loose stones, the three followed Yeshua to a wider, smoother path, which led gradually upwards. The Master kept a little way ahead, carefully guiding them as the path grew narrower and steeper. James, panting somewhat, was amazed to see how agile the Master was, hoisting himself between two high rocks, then waiting wordlessly to help his clumsy disciples through the gap – just like a shepherd rescuing a couple of stranded sheep – a jutting stone, a grassy tow-hold – ever higher, following their Lord.

Unimagined breathtaking vistas of distant sea opened out before their astonished gaze. It became a day of surprises – soft green hollows, dangerous sloping rock faces; tiny mountain flowers of blue, white and purple; spiny thorn bushes and impossible ankle-twisting clefts.

At last, the summit. A flat grassy table with a platform of grey rocks near the edge. There was just one way up or down.

As the little company broke bread, the first stars began to appear. Darkness approached swiftly. John shivered as he looked around, glad of the Master's presence in this remote, lofty place.

Far below them, the Sea of Galilee shone like a jewel as the distant hills of Judea began to merge together in the fading light.

There was a slight dip in the grass where the three weary fishermen sat. They had been climbing since morning, a glorious experience behind such a Leader, filling them with confidence. The views had been spectacular with many a gasp of surprise, but pauses had been brief. Ever urgent, the Master's silhouette would appear at the next corner, the next awkward lift. Now they were exhausted and ready to rest.

Instead of joining them, their Lord was seen moving in the shadows towards the rocky platform, his dark outline soon appearing at the top, kneeling in prayer to his heavenly Father. James wondered sleepily where the Master's energy came from. Peter was already sleeping. John continued to watch his Master with wide eyes, knowing that his Lord was gaining fresh strength for his task right now. But in a few more moments John too closed his eyes, while the Master continued in prayer.

Something woke them – a light; brighter, sharper than moonlight. Awkwardly the three staggered to their feet, clinging to each other. An unbearable glory was radiating from the Master himself. His whole being seemed made of light. He stood, his radiant face turned upward to Heaven – love, glory and light in perfect harmony. His very clothes seemed transparent.

At once there were two figures standing with him, outshone by the Lord's brilliance. Snatches of talk drifted to the three concerning the Master's "departure", to take place at Jerusalem, by which he would "draw all men" to himself. There was no question as to who the two visitors were. Their authority left no doubt. But even great Moses and Elijah bowed as they took their leave of the Master's royal majesty.

Peter stepped forward and shouted, reluctant to allow the wonderful scene to come to an end. His words were drowned in the glory of the moment.

A bright cloud suddenly appeared among the stars above them. As it descended, the hills below the mountaintop and the grassy summit around them took on the appearance of a beautiful dawn. The three companions were enveloped in its billowing folds.

An awesome, heavenly whiteness covered them, blotting out all their thoughts and surroundings. As James, Peter and John fell on to their faces in terror, a calm clear voice was heard from somewhere around and within them.

"This is my beloved Son! In him I am well pleased! Hear him!"

Suddenly the vision, the blinding radiance, the cloud – all were gone. James, Peter and John opened their eyes and saw no one but Yeshua.

"Rise up," he said. "Do not be afraid."

The way down seemed like a dream. Every damp rock they touched, each tuft of grass beneath their sandaled feet seemed unreal in the pink and grey shadows of the approaching day. A blue haze hung in the wooded valley below the mountain, vanishing as the sun's glaring rim appeared over their shoulders. At one point the Master, very ordinary now, with green smudges on his clothes from helping his companions to negotiate tight corners, told the three that they must keep the vision to themselves "until I am risen from the dead", a saying that left them wondering all over again.

At last they returned to level ground. James drank gratefully from a wayside spring. Then he looked up. People were running towards them, among whom he recognised Judas and Matthew. The village people all bowed and saluted the Master as the crowd gathered around them.

One older man stepped forward, almost in tears. "My son," he cried, "is tormented day and night. A devil is forever trying to throw him into the fire or into the river. I can't do anything with him!"

The Master glanced meaningfully at his confused disciples.

"They couldn't help," said the man. "They failed each time. We were hoping that you..."

Yeshua lifted himself up and surveyed the crowd, taking in the whole scene. Visibly disturbed, he said, "O faithless people – how long shall I be with you? How long must I endure you? Bring him to me."

A writhing, foaming bundle collapsed at Yeshua's feet, its arms and legs distorted and thrashing wildly. A more pathetic creature had never been presented to the Lord throughout his ministry.

Yeshua spoke immediately and sharply. "Out – stay out! Go!"

Dreadful noises and contortions followed these commands. All at once the boy lay still. There came a hush. Yeshua stepped forward and touched him, speaking quietly. Slowly the lad sat up, throwing his arm over his frightened eyes and gazing around in wonder at the ranks of shocked faces.

The Life of Yeshua

Another word from the Master and the people began to turn away towards their homes.

The sun was high in the sky now. Yeshua the Master, with one shepherd's glance at his twelve, moved off towards the southern road. Behind them all was John, normally so close to his Lord, but now deep in thought. The Master was heading for distant Jerusalem. What might happen there? John could be certain of one thing; the Lord knew and was himself the focus of some wonderful plan of God, which, seemingly, would echo around the whole world.

But what were the heavenly words they had heard in those moments of glory? The Lord's "departure" – what did that mean? And why did the beloved Master speak so often about a "cross"?

"My beloved Son..." The words which John had heard in the cloud warmed his heart. He quickened his pace. *Keep following, keep trusting.* They were on their way to Jerusalem. Everything would be answered in Jerusalem.

Chapter Fourteen

Capernaum was all activity and bustle. Chatter and laughter filled the air. All front doors were open, the streets crowded with laden donkeys, men fastening cords, mothers packing fruit and bread into saddlebags, dusty tents being flapped open, shaken and examined for holes. Children dashed around, clamouring to take a favourite toy, and one thought in everyone's mind – Jerusalem! The whole town, it seemed, would be going up to the city in one long, happy, psalm-singing pilgrimage.

Feast of Tabernacles was one of the happiest times of the year. Long ago Moses had instructed the people of Israel to spend a week's holiday each year living, not in ordinary houses, but in camps or cabins made of poles and leafy branches, so that they might never forget the hardships of their ancestors as they journeyed through the empty wilderness for forty long years.

In Jerusalem the Pharisees and priests watched the floods of people ebbing and flowing around the shining pavements of the Temple and the busy, colourful markets. Hatred burned in their hearts as they planned the capture of that Yeshua of Nazareth. "He is sure to be here," said a young, black-bearded elder. "Be vigilant! This time we shall have him."

The Life of Yeshua

Annas, the old retired High Priest, shuffled forward and joined his fellows at the high window. Below them a surging throng of humanity, waving, singing psalms, flowed towards the Temple gates, some even pausing in the crush to kiss the very stones in their joy. However oppressed they were by the Pharisees, however pushed around by the Romans, one thing they knew which no one could change – the God of Abraham was still their God and he would never leave them. Their paeans of joy filled the dusty air.

Annas turned to the serving priests in their smooth robes, their faces eager and set to do their worst. He raised his finger. "Do you hear what these ignorant Galileans are singing? 'Hosanna to the Son of David!' Listen to me..." He focused his gaze upon each one in turn. "Do not rejoice until the lion is in the net! Just one word from Yeshua of Nazareth and he could stand at the head of an army. Then down will fall Rome like eagles and we shall all be destroyed!"

"Yes..." Caiaphas followed his father-in-law's gaze through the open window. "Far better," he continued shrewdly, "that one man should die than the nation perish." His face broke into a cruel smile.

"Perhaps something will turn up."

On their way to Jerusalem, the Lord's company had to pass through Jericho to renew their provisions. The disciples hoped to make the best speed through this city, which had a bad history, but the Master was soon recognised as they hurried through the crowded streets and markets. The following crowd grew continually larger; not hostile, more like strayed sheep finding a shepherd. At last – the City gate. Peter increased his step as they approached the echoing arch. The mixed crowd still followed, but the Lord did not even glance at the array of muttering beggars crouched against the wall holding out their palms. God had a cause against Jericho.

At once a cry was heard behind them. Bartimaeus could see nothing, but his ears were good. They had to be! Daily he sat among the beggars outside Jericho's gate, listening. He seldom raised his voice, leaving that to others, content to hold out his hands and listen. Even the sighted beggars would sometimes say, "What do you hear, Bartimaeus?" He could distinguish between the plod of carthorses and the regular hollow chop of a cavalry charger being led through the gate. He could tell by the rustle of clothes and the scrape of a sandal whether rich or poor were passing – and the difference between a shuffling mob and a squad of soldiers. He also picked up snatches of unguarded conversation. No one worried much about beggars!

Bartimaeus also knew in his heart that one day God's Messiah, the Son of David, would come, and he had his own ideas about that! One hope he nurtured in his breast. When the Son of David came, he, Bartimaeus, would receive his sight and join Messiah's army. Bartimaeus prayed and knew in his heart that his day would come. And so he waited.

On that cool morning there came the sound of many feet. Snatches of echoing talk drifted to him as a large company of travellers passed beneath the arch of Jericho's gate. Bartimaeus leaped to his feet. "Who is it?"

"Yeshua of Nazareth is passing by."

Bartimaeus' heart leaped with sudden hope. His day had come! Act now, he must, or allow the wonderful moment of opportunity to pass forever. "Yeshua! Yeshua – Son of David! Wait! Stop!" He had no idea where to look.

The whole multitude fell upon him with hissed warnings and rebukes. "Not that! Never let the Romans hear you say that!"

A dour Roman guard at the gate, well turned out with gleaming helmet and spear, was already taking an interest.

Bartimaeus thrust their protests aside, leaping and dancing in his dark world. "It is true! Yeshua, you Son of David, Israel's promised Messiah – wait!"

The multitude looked for the Master himself to rebuke or ignore the blind man's cries. Instead, Yeshua halted.

In the stunned silence Bartimaeus' forbidden cries echoed around the city walls. "Have mercy upon me – Saviour, Israel's Messiah!"

Yeshua looked at him across the crowd and spoke.

"Cheer up!" someone shouted. "He's calling you."

Bartimaeus made one joyous leap in the dark, casting his outer cloak aside as he did so, in the clear knowledge that if he was wrong about Yeshua, he might never find that precious garment again. Full of confidence, the blind man marched forward in the dark, only stopping when he felt the hard road beneath his feet.

A voice like none other spoke at his elbow. "What would you have me do for you?"

"Lord," Bartimaeus replied to the unseen presence, "I desire that I might receive my sight."

"Go your way," the presence replied. "Your faith has made you whole."

Instantly, Bartimaus' life was filled with light.

The first thing he saw was the glory of God in the face of Yeshua of Nazareth.

Chapter Fifteen

Judas Iscariot was confused. Why did the Master keep disappearing? Was it treachery? The weary disciples were laughing again. Who were they laughing at – *me?* Why did the Master continually refuse to gather an army together?

Judas could not remember why he had begun to follow the Rabbi in the first place. Soon it was too late. He was so surprised when the Lord not only chose him to serve among the twelve but also to become Treasurer and keep the bag. Amazing luck! Judas' one ambition was to line his own pocket by any means possible. What an opportunity! This was why he continued following with the company – a chain forged personally by the Lord. But things were becoming urgent now. Months had gone by, many opportunities to rouse the people had been lost and Judas was growing impatient. Unknown to him, his Master Yeshua knew all about it. Crisis point came not many days later.

As they neared Jerusalem, breaking their journey each Sabbath to visit a local synagogue, a Pharisee approached James.

"Your Master is invited to my supper," he said smoothly. "Would you convey the message?"

James could see exactly what this meant. A large well-swept courtyard attached to an expensive house.

Laid out to seat – or recline – several groups of people, rich and poor, upon cushions around linen tablecloths, rather like an informal picnic. The top table, where the Pharisee host sat, would have the finest cutlery and places, the salt, and the best attention of the servants. Below the salt, the groups would be arranged in order of diminishing status, those seated nearest the entrance often having grubby linen, threadbare cushions and the poorest selection of the dishes. The Lord and his disciples would likely be placed in the lowest corner of all, to be served last. After supper the Pharisees would begin a loud discussion on some controversial topic, and try to involve Yeshua of Nazareth and trap him in his words.

James knew what his Master's reply would be without asking. "Our Master will be pleased to accept," he affirmed.

On the evening of the supper, the host welcomed his fellow Pharisees with an elaborate kiss and personally washed their dusty feet in scented water.

By the time Yeshua and the twelve stood beneath the arched entrance, the servant carrying the bowl and towel had departed, while the host held loud and incessant conversation with his cronies.

It was all so obvious – the neglect of the Nazarene, the obsequious fuss made of the rich guests, all designed to humiliate the twelve and their Master. Thomas and Thaddeus indeed were hot with embarrassment.

The supper itself, however, passed off uneventfully, with only the bustle of servants, the wafting smell of hot food, the clink of cutlery and the occasional nervous laugh. Most people present were aware of the animosity between the two main parties. Yeshua's calmness, however, seemed to affect everyone nearby, including the servants.

It was during the fruit course that the disruption happened. The atmosphere had grown increasingly tense. The Pharisees already had their heads together planning the open questions they would throw at the Master as soon as supper was cleared away.

Suddenly, a woman's voice was heard at the archway, tearful and distraught, throwing off the servants who tried to restrain her. Bursting into the courtyard and shaking away her tears, she looked around clutching a beautiful box to her chest. Judas recognised this and never took his eyes from it – a white alabaster casket, perhaps an heirloom, and originally from ancient Egypt. Judas knew it must be beyond price. How could he get his hands on it? His mind whirled in panic.

A great gasp travelled around the company. The entire supper party sat back in horror, recognising the woman as an infamous follower of felons, Romans and every evil element in society – erect and proud, her beautiful hair piled on her head in the latest Roman fashion. They all knew her and avoided her in street and market. But no one had ever seen her like this. Shattered and racked with sobs, her deranged hair hanging in long red streaks across her shoulders. She ran to find the Master seated among his friends and swayed above him.

Judas could hardly restrain himself at what happened next. He had been thinking that possession of that alabaster box and its contents would set him up for life. Now he almost leaped to his feet in horror as the woman wrenched the seals of the box apart and began pouring the exquisite liquid contents over the Master's bare feet and over his head. Still sobbing, she began lovingly wiping the Master's feet with the tangled, knotted mass of her once unrivalled hair.

A heavy, adorable, indescribably beautiful perfume welled up around them, spreading its fragrance across the whole courtyard. The perfume was pure nard, an exclusive compound used for anointing Egyptian Kings and Queens. Some of the company began to murmur in delight as the vapours reached them in the walled court.

The Pharisees were white with shock over the woman's actions, blaming Yeshua for encouraging such a scene.

The Master stayed as he was, speaking soothingly to the woman whom he knew had repented of her old life and done away with her pride and her beautiful hair. She knew that somehow Yeshua himself held the key to her salvation and that the Pharisees would take his life. Her dearest treasure had been poured out as a token for all to see, of her love and gratitude to God.

In the silence the entire company heard the Master's authoritative and comforting words. "Go in peace. Your sins are all forgiven."

Judas leaped up, trying to shake away the noxious fumes that filled his nostrils – the scent of a vanished fortune. This was the final indignity that faithful Judas could stand. Was nothing sacred? Trembling and drawing

The Life of Yeshua

deep, unwilling breaths of those mocking fumes, he heard his own voice, shrill and unnatural like an upset child.

"What is the purpose of this waste?"

Every eye turned upon him. Not a finger moved. Two other people nodded in uncertain agreement. The whole company waited for Judas to speak again. Turning his eyes wide with rage upon the woman, he heard his own voice again, sounding like that of a bad actor learning his lines.

"Why was this not sold for great money and given to the poor?" He found it almost impossible to utter the last five words. His meaning was obvious to all. He glared at the dismayed woman.

"Leave her alone!" It was the Master's voice in a tone normally reserved for subduing demons.

All eyes turned away from the smouldering, cringing Judas and towards the Master. His next words were unforgettable, as was the whole scene in that heavily perfumed assembly.

"The poor are always with you. Why wait until now to do them good? I shall not always be with you. She has done a memorable work, anointing me for my burial."

Unknown to the supper-party, they had not only witnessed the repentance of a notorious sinner but also a solemn ceremony, unique in the history of Israel and the world. Now Yeshua's path would take him to Jerusalem, where his sheep would be scattered and their Shepherd done away.

Judas stood speechless. Some strong restraint within him snapped like a rotten rope. So that was what the

Master was about – pointless, empty religion. No high financial position for faithful Judas in a coming Kingdom. No army to command; no captured Roman trophies to pore over – all gone in one puff of scented smoke.

Judas glanced behind him wildly. He would keep his own counsel. He was determined to gain something, a consolation prize. Those priests in the City would pay to know how and where they could lay their hands on the prophet from Nazareth. Pay well, too – he would see to that! Iron resolve seized him as the stunned company poured out into the perfumed night.

Chapter Sixteen

The rocky road down from Bethany winds around the southern slopes of the Mount of Olives, where it meets the road to Jerusalem. The Lord and his disciples joined the highway at the same time as a great company of people and families on pilgrimage from the north, from Magdala and Dalmanutha. Cries of joyful recognition rent the air as they saw Yeshua, almost enfolding him in their arms and bearing him along. The disciples recognised so many happy faces among that moving throng, of those who had been healed by the Master, but there was no frantic clamour this time. Many began to clap in broken applause as a sign of their joy at meeting him. Some began to sing the psalms of David, quietly and reverently at first, with gentle harmony, as they bore Yeshua and his disciples along with them.

"Hosanna!" they sang. "Save, O Lord, we pray. Send now prosperity. How blessed is he who comes in the name of the Lord! We have blessed you, the One from the House of the Lord. God is the Lord!"

Not much farther to go now. As the song faded away, the multitude with Yeshua in their midst came within sight of their destination, the City and the Temple of God.

Near the village of Bethphage, the Master halted. Choosing two disciples he told them, "Go into the village.

You will find an ass tethered with her colt. Loose and bring them. Say, 'The Lord needs them.'"

Soon the two returned, leading the animals. "The owners practically forced them upon us!"

The thinner, darker donkey was the mother, but the un-ridden colt was a magnificent creature, pale in colour with long silky ears and a beautiful head. "Fit for a King," someone murmured. It was indeed clear to everyone that the day had dawned in which Yeshua the Master would ride into Jerusalem upon a King's beast with all the dignity of the promised Son of David, and evident acceptance of every royal title he had avoided when offered it by men.

The disciples threw their cloaks over the young donkey's back. The Master mounted and the procession advanced, growing to almost frightening proportions and yet all in good order with arms lifted in welcome, snatches of songs and psalms filling the air.

The real celebration began a mile or more from the City, where the multitude met a great concourse of pilgrims coming out of Jerusalem, having heard that the Prophet from Nazareth was on his way.

It seemed as if the entire population of Judah and Israel lined the way, cheering and singing. The throng had to surge through an avenue of graceful palm trees with heavy, fan-like branches of deep green; so heavy, the trees themselves seemed to bow low in the presence of the Master as he progressed upon his noble steed.

Younger men raced among the trees, cutting down the great curtained branches, lining the Master's route

The Life of Yeshua

with a waving green arch, moving in time with the chanting, which by now had become an organized defiant roar. Every throat among that waving greenery chanted and sang to the skies.

"Hosanna! Hosanna to the King – the King of Israel! Praise God for the Son of David, coming in his name. Hosanna!"

There was no going back now. The Master sat bareheaded and erect. Completely calm and in control, no look of regal pride on his face, just love for the people and evidence of a deep secret sorrow. Indeed, at one high place in the road he paused and wept for the City waiting to receive him.

At the City gates the cheering, rejoicing and palm-waving were at their most intense. Not a hundred yards from that wide, towering arch surrounded with cheering crowds and waving greenery, three irate priests elbowed their rough way through to the Master and grabbed the donkey's head.

"Rabbi! Do you hear what your disciples are shouting? Stop them before there's big trouble!"

Only the closest to them heard the Master's reply. "Truly, I tell you – if these are stopped, the very stones will cry out."

The cheering crowds surged on, leaving the Pharisees standing. John, walking just behind the donkey, caught a sudden waft of perfume from the Master's clothes, and his song died away as he remembered the Master's words just two nights before.

The next hour became no more than a blur in John's memory. The tumultuous scenes at the City gate – the absence of the Romans, ever watchful in the background; the helpless Pharisees and priests. The determined expression of Yeshua, as he dismounted and in all that mêlée ordered the donkeys to be returned at once; his march up the stony road to the Temple, where the entrance courts were jammed with the multicoloured awnings of market stalls, sellers of lambs, doves, money-changers, all sanctioned (and probably financed) by the Temple priests. The mingled cries, shouts, cheers and animal noises as Yeshua, in righteous wrath, tore down awnings, threw tables of money in every direction, overturned stalls, and upended benches.

The jingle of coin on hard pavement and the flutter of escaping birds filled the air. Stallholders threw their arms across their startled faces before fleeing for the lives.

Yeshua's powerful tones followed them across the wreckage. "This is my Father's house – a place of prayer for all nations. You have turned it into a den of thieves!"

"He called God 'his Father'," a bystander noted, as they hurried away, "acting as if he owned the Temple himself."

"Perhaps he does..." another finished thoughtfully.

Judas was missing. While the smoke from the pilgrims' fires still hung in the dawn air he had stolen hurriedly away from the lodgings at Bethany and taken the high road to Jerusalem. He had important business with the Sanhedrin, the religious Council, whose one ambition was to trap and do away with Yeshua of Nazareth.

A servant knocked gently on the High Priest's study door. It was early, but Caiaphas was around, awaiting other members of the Council.

"A... err... gentleman to see Your Grace."

At a sign Judas entered, cautiously glancing around.

Caiaphas came straight to the point. "You are one of his disciples."

"I *was*," Judas lied. He became aware of other shadowy figures entering the room, bowing facetiously in the direction of the High Priest, who ignored them. Caiaphas wanted action, or this traitor would be thrown out.

"What's your business?"

"How much will you pay me if I betray him to you?" The direct approach was best – no names were necessary.

Excellent, thought Caiaphas. He glanced at the Sanhedrin, each man trying to suppress a smile of triumph.

"I can tell you exactly where he will be and at what time," Judas blurted out. "Away from the crowds," he added significantly.

Caiaphas gestured to a clerk, who placed a clanking pair of scales upon the table and a sealed bag of money – real silver, each coin worth a month's wages. Watching Judas' eyes, Caiaphas dipped into the bag, allowing the precious coins to run through his fingers. "Thirty," he said suddenly. "No more!"

He knew his man! Judas stuttered and his mouth opened wide. His price had been fifty! The scales clanked down as the weights were removed. He was lost.

"Done," Judas said. Stepping forward he poured the thirty pieces of silver from the tray into his pocket. A few words more sufficed. "Bring lanterns and spears," he concluded. "The one I shall kiss is your man." Then he was gone.

Chapter Seventeen

Passover – a bitter-sweet time of the year when scattered families gathered together. James and John looked back each year at the time of spring flowers to boyhood Passover evenings, when all the family from the oldest to the youngest would gather around the largest table and see upon its white cloth the dishes, bowls and little porcelain pots, only taken from the cupboard once a year. The eldest grandfather or uncle would sit at the head, carve and serve the whole roasted lamb – a real luxury in most homes – and snap the unleavened wafer-bread to pass around. Watered wine in a special cup was passed from hand to hand for all to taste and the grandfather would unroll the family scriptures. He would then lead in prayer, thanking God for all his beautiful creation and everyone would say, "Amen."

After another taste of wine, another family elder would give thanks for God's rescue of Israel from dreadful slavery in Egypt. Dishes of bitter-tasting herbs and salt water to dip them in were served next, and more wafer-bread spread with the brick-red fig purée, to remind the families of the hard work in the Egyptian brick fields.

At a certain point in the meal, a mother would prompt her youngest child, and while all the guests watched and waited the boy would shyly ask, if he could, "What do we mean by this service?"

The grandfather would fold his hands and begin the true history of Israel, how God had made a pathway through the Red Sea for the escaping people, given them Moses as their leader and guided them through the wilderness, and how everything on that Passover table had something to teach them, especially the whole roast lamb.

Happy memories – and tonight was to be the third Passover supper with Yeshua at the head – the first time also that they would be keeping Passover behind barred doors, somewhere in Jerusalem.

Passover evenings were sweet and cool as the twelve lay concealed among the olive branches in the Garden of Gethsemane. Glorious fresh nights beneath the fiery constellations spread in such profusion across the dark sky. At dusk a dark red Passover moon would show its rim in the furthest east, growing brighter as it rose to pass in queenly procession through the constellations, putting them all to shame. But that was for later. This very night was Passover. Where should they prepare for their supper?

"Go into the City," said the Master, "and watch for a man carrying a pitcher of water on his head. Follow him. He will have our room waiting."

Judas was still Treasurer. He turned fidgety when Peter and John asked him for money to buy the necessary items for the supper.

Carrying their wares purchased from the market, they were shown up a dark, creaking staircase leading to a door which they pushed open. The room was filled with

The Life of Yeshua

daylight from two open casements which looked out on to the busy streets below. The room was large but bare except for a long table, several wooden chairs and two large earthenware jars filled with fresh water from the well outside. The place was clean and comfortable, yet the two companions felt uneasy. Their Lord was under the watchful eye of his enemies in this City. This could be no ordinary family Passover meal. They had been instructed to buy only the bare essentials for the supper. The whole roast lamb would be fetched last of all.

Even tonight, of all nights, the twelve made a concerted rush for the stairs, pushing and treading on each other's feet, hoping to gain the most favoured places near the Master around the table. This only gained for them a lecture from the Master and a reminder that the first shall be last. John and Judas, who had not joined the rush, were each given a place beside the Lord.

Yeshua, so very solemn, waited until all their attention was upon him. Something had been forgotten. The disciples looked guiltily at each other. A chair with a clean towel and a bowl stood to one side unnoticed. In their scramble for the most 'honourable' seats, each had expected that the next man should do the humblest job of all, that of the foot-washing servant. No one moved.

Quietly, Yeshua arose from his place at the head. While his twelve watched in horror, he stripped to the waist, poured water into the basin and knelt before the first disciple. Nothing was heard except for the trickle of water and the Master's gentle invitation as he knelt before each mortified disciple. That the incomparably greatest among them should stoop to do, with love, such a task destroyed their pride forever, and shone a light upon so much of Yeshua's teaching over the months that they had ignored – until Peter's turn came.

Recent memories of mistakes and rebukes still troubled him. As the Lord knelt before him, Peter withdrew. "Lord – you will never wash my feet!" The thought was unbearable.

Still kneeling, the Lord looked up at Peter. "If I do not wash you, Peter, you have no part with me!"

Peter shrank. *Another mistake! What a lesson! All need to be washed by the Christ to come into fellowship with Him!* "Lord, then wash me all over!"

Placing Peter's foot in the soft towel, the Lord replied, "You are clean already. The feet have daily contact with the earth – those are the parts that need to be washed."

The Lord dressed and sat down. But before his prayer he looked at them again and said, "What I do for you now, you must do for each other."

In silence, they all took their places again. But there was worse to come. They waited for the Lord to bless the salt, the fruit and all the joyful things that grew from the earth, but instead the Master paused and looked at each one with the most sorrowful expression.

"Most truly, I tell you – one of you here with me will betray me."

A gasp of disbelief went around the table. Faces turned to each other in amazement, then to the Lord.

"Lord, is it I?" "Lord... can it be... me?" "Lord, surely not me!"

"It is one of you who dips his bread into the dish with me."

Unnoticed in the confusion, Yeshua looked full into the shifty eyes of Iscariot. "Do what you have to do. Go quickly!"

Judas fled from the room, clattered down the stairs and vanished into the night.

Only the Master knew his errand. In the agony of the moment the others believed that he had been sent out to fetch something.

The dreadful moment seemed to fade away in the general activity. The hot broth was finished and the meal proper began. The Master prayed as the first cup was passed around, the Cup of Thankfulness. After this the unleavened wafer-bread was broken and spread with the red fig purée. But this time, after the Master gave thanks he took a fresh loaf and began to break it saying, "This bread is my body, broken for you. Whenever you do this, always remember me."

As the broken bread was passed around, they wondered what it all meant. A betrayal – and the Master's body broken for them! Is that what John Baptist meant when he cried, pointing to Yeshua, "Behold – the Lamb of God who takes away the sin of the world!"?

It fell to John to ask the question, "Why is this night so special?"

The Master, as head, retold the tales of Moses and Pharoah, dwelling much on the Passover Lamb and

Moses' instruction to take its blood before it was roasted, and paint the doorposts of the Jewish houses with it, as a sign that their dwellings had a special protection from God's judgement on the night that he would punish the Egyptians for all their cruelty to Israel.

The eleven listened, absorbed, as if it were the first time they had heard the history. Yeshua, as ever, taught from his own authority, unlike the scribes. It seemed almost as if he had been present on that very night. Then there was another surprise. With supper over, the Master took the last cup of wine to bless and give thanks. Having prayed, he lifted the cup in both hands and looked at his eleven. "This cup is the sign of a new covenant between yourselves and God. This wine represents my blood, which is the seal of the new covenant. My own blood will be poured out for you, that all your sins may be forgiven. Whenever you drink this cup, do it in remembrance of me."

They heard his words. Their full meaning would become clear later.

The whole of Israel's national life had been founded upon the Passover lamb as a sign that God had cleared their sin and adopted Abraham's family as his own. Now, this very night, a new covenant was to spring out of the old and stand beside it! So their Yeshua was the Lamb of God after all, even the Lamb for the whole world.

As the eleven gazed in awe at Yeshua at the head of the table, a light began to dawn in their understanding. They glanced at each other. *What a mixed company! And yet, each one chosen to serve.*

With no idea of the future, or even of coming events this night, they knew one thing – that they would be the first to travel in lands near and far, telling out the great news of sins forgiven for all who would believe in their Yeshua, the Son of God from Heaven.

Waves of God's love enveloped them as they each, in turn, took the cup. As John took it into his hands, the full meaning of it struck him; his breath stopped. It meant that the Master must surrender his life and die, like the Passover Lamb they had eaten.

John noticed, for the first time, the empty place beside the Master. Where had Judas gone and not returned, before the Lord had drawn his own into the new covenant?

Outside in the street below, a cohort of Roman guards marched past, glancing up as the Master led the disciples in a psalm of joy and victory.

Chapter Eighteen

Staying behind to blow out the lamps, John looked around the dark and empty room. Moonlight streamed through the two casements on to the bare, white tablecloth. He wanted to memorise every precious moment of this last Passover spent with the Beloved.

They filed across the brook Kidron by the wooden bridge, as ever following the Master and heading for their haven deep within the garden of Gethsemane, a place of olive trees, dry grassy dells and comforting shadows. Tonight the Lord signed for Peter, James and John to follow him deeper into the olive wood, where piles of fragrant leaf-mould lay stacked.

He spoke to them in the shadows, in the flickering shade, his eyes shining from a face filled with such horror that they had never imagined before.

"My heart is filled with deepest anguish. Stay and watch with me."

Seeing the Lord fall to his knees in that stark, unrelenting moonlight reminded the three of their time on the mountain, when they had seen the glory of the Lord. Now they saw him in a different light, an agony of some dreadful unseen battle between good and evil. Fragments of his prayer drifted to them on the still air.

"Father, if it be possible... this cup... your will..."

The Life of Yeshua

The Master had given his flock the sweet cup which would bring them life. What was this bitter cup that he must now drink alone? As before, the three, so deeply moved to see their Master so affected, drifted into sleep...

Suddenly, a movement and his voice: "Wake up! My betrayer is here!"

A crackle of twigs and branches and the eleven were with him. Below them the City wall, Temple and palaces shone white. The ravine further down was black. Judas had already led his party of Temple police and officers to the fringe of the sheltering trees. They had crossed the bridge and their line of bobbing flames, the glint of helmet and spear-point began to thread into the deeper approaches of the olive wood. Boldly, the Lord walked out into a clearing to meet them. The party halted in surprise.

Yeshua stood before a circle of torch-lit, uncertain faces. As ever, he took command. "Whom do you seek?"

A familiar figure, grim and unkempt stepped into the circle of light. "Hail, Master!" said Judas, greeting Yeshua with a rough embrace.

"Judas," replied the Lord, "do you betray the Son of Man with a kiss?" Then, turning to the hesitating band of guards, he raised his voice. "I asked, whom do you seek?"

"Yeshua of Nazareth," a voice replied.

The Master stepped between the torch-bearers and his own wavering disciples. "I AM!" The words came with an unexpected power and authority, far beyond their own.

The burly spearmen clutched at each other and fell to the ground.

The Master spoke again. "I have told you that I am he. Let these others go."

They made a sudden rush for him. A crash and a cry, and the disciples fled in several directions, pursued half-heartedly by some of the guards.

The sound of the chase faded away. The disciples knew those woods well. The tramp of marching feet diminished in the opposite direction. The swiftly enacted scene was over. The Master had surrendered to his foes. The clearing stood empty.

A rustling in the bushes – John emerged, glancing all around. In a moment Peter was beside him. A quick greeting, then together a race among grotesque shapes and twisting paths, pausing to point breathlessly at the procession of bobbing torch flames crossing the bridge below them. Soundlessly, commando-fashion they followed, dashing from behind a tree to race across the bridge, past the vineyard and around the building where their supper had taken place.

A grassy path, a broken wooden gate – the High Priest's garden! Known to the family, John knew where he was going. A shaft of light from a side door, John's silhouette beckoning to Peter – then he was gone.

Peter had no desire to follow John into a strange house, especially that of Caiaphas and Annas. He looked around him. He was in a courtyard, busy for this time of night. *Must be because of the Master. Best to blend in with the company,* thought Peter, having no idea what to do next, just wanting to show some kind of loyalty to Yeshua.

The moon was setting behind the palace. Peter shivered in the cold air. A good fire blazed in the middle of the courtyard. A couple of off-duty Temple guards threw on another dead branch, warming their hands. Casually, Peter sidled towards them. *Ah, that's better...*

A servant girl came out with a bowl of hot drink and a cup. The crowd around the fire grew. Peter held out his hand as the girl passed. Giving him the cup, she looked at him curiously in the half light as he returned it empty.

"Surely," she said, "you were with Yeshua of Nazareth."

"Not me," said Peter instinctively. She was only a girl. "You've made a mistake."

She marched off with her empty bowl, head in air. "I don't make mistakes!"

Peter's blood ran cold. He was trapped. Another servant girl was watching him, having overheard the conversation. She drew nearer.

"You *were* with him!" Her voice was pert, sharply accusing. "You followed him like a shadow."

"I've never met the man, I tell you!" Peter's voice echoed around the dark courtyard. Some guards moved around to his side of the fire and surveyed him minutely.

"You're a Galilean, one of his band."

"Your speech gives you away," added the second, "if nothing else does."

Peter Marks

Peter, crouching, rose angrily to his feet. "I tell you I don't know who or what you're talking about!" His eyes flashed fiercely. He was a big man. The soldiers retreated.

At that moment a door opened in the balcony above them. Guarded by two soldiers, Yeshua came out. Before entering another door he paused. Peter's eyes met his.

Realising that Peter was not following, John closed the servant's door and hurried down the corridor, brushing twigs and leaves from his clothes. He was determined to stay near the master for as long as he could.

Shabby, tousled Pharisees were arriving, disturbed at their rest, yet delighted to know that the Nazarene was, at last, apprehended. They would be in no mood to compromise.

Glancing up the corridor, John tried to hide near the door behind which the proceedings were already taking place. He heard hollow footsteps, the scrape of chairs as the Council took their seats, followed by the official, nasal voice of Caiaphas reading a charge – strange, hesitant statements. John pressed his ear to the door, struggling to pick up some word.

Large doors suddenly broke open and the Master was led out and given into the hands of a Roman officer and four men in bright armour. That, John knew, meant a walk up a flight of marble stairs, crossing a floor of coloured tiles and standing before Pilate the Roman governor.

The Life of Yeshua

Sometime later, John joined a shifting multitude below the Governor's gallery. The shouting and bellowing of the mob whipped up by the priests was unbearable, and when Pilate appeared and cried out, "Shall I release the King of the Jews?" a tumult arose, dust was thrown and the cry went up, "Not him! Barabbas! We want Barabbas!"

John turned away and wept.

He knew what that meant for his beloved Master.

Chapter Nineteen

The well-trodden pathway to Calvary began at the back gate of Pilate's prison. It was a winding, stone-strewn stumbling way, along which a prisoner never returned. It followed the foot of the white-washed city walls, a dry, hopeless path, crossing no brook.

In one prison cell the rebel leader Barabbas crouched, waiting his moment to tread that path, bearing his heavy cross. Instead there came a sudden clank of Roman armour, a jingle of keys, and the iron door to his rock-walled cell swung back. Was this the moment? No. It was relief beyond words! The guards' officer raised his baton threateningly.

"Get out!"

Barabbas flinched. "Wha..."

"Get out!" the Roman repeated, aiming a vicious kick.

Barabbas fled, asking no more questions.

In an adjoining hall, Yeshua, the promised King of Israel, was being mocked by the half-dressed off duty soldiers. They had woven a kingly crown for him from sharp thorn bushes and rammed it over his forehead. Blood was running down his cheeks. Their jeers were interrupted by an officer standing beneath the arch.

"Take the prisoner out. His cross is prepared!"

The Life of Yeshua

Not many miles away an elderly woman named Huldah sat alone in the shade of a green tree, mixing bread. Pausing in her work, she looked up. From the pure blue sky a cold breeze touched her cheek. She gazed deep into the rapidly changing face of the heavens and thought of Yeshua of Nazareth.

"Today," she said aloud, "is the day of his glory!"

John followed the Lord to the end, knowing that Yeshua's road as Lamb of God led beyond Jerusalem. Calvary was a hill outside the City wall.

Bruised and beaten, the Lord bore his Roman cross to that place, there to be crucified between two members of Barabbas' gang.

A strange darkness fell, but no storm followed. The family group at the foot of the cross clung to each other in sorrow. Their Yeshua, whose words were Life and Truth, whose deeds were God's own, releasing sufferers from bondage, Yeshua, Son of God Most High – was no more.

Tender hands would come and wrap him in a linen sheet among posies of myrrh. He would be laid in a room cut from the rock, close by a lovely garden. Friendly hands would quietly close the door – a large, round stone – upon all their hopes.

But God had greater plans.

Chapter Twenty

What a glorious spring morning! A warm sun shone over the garden through a rising mist. Flowers everywhere – dew-soaked shrubs breaking into blossom – pink showers of petals among the blue and red anemones, yellow daffodils livening the grey stones, daisies growing in the crevices of the low walls among the clumps of moss. The whole world seemed to be singing, "Alive! Alive! Wake up – look around!"

The only sadness seemed to follow the five women bringing flowers and gifts to leave at Yeshua's grave. As they carried their baskets, they talked about their problem – who would roll the stone away from the door? They hurried across a patch of wet grass, down three steps, then clung to each other in dismay.

"The stone – it's gone!"

"It's fallen over. How – who…?"

Then a cry. "He's gone – his place is empty!"

Five grey-clad figures fled in disarray from the garden, leaving their precious baskets overturned and scattered.

The door of the little lodging burst open. Startled, Peter and John looked up.

The Life of Yeshua

"He's gone – been taken away!" The gasping women poured out their story.

A chair crashed to the floor as the two friends ran outside heading full pelt for the garden where the Master had been laid to rest. Peter, more cumbersome, watched John's lithe figure disappear among the tall foliage bordering the garden. By the time Peter caught up, John was standing quietly by the fallen stone, looking into the tomb. He appeared quite calm.

Peter dashed heavily past his friend into the small cave and looked around. The bed was empty, the linen cover tidily folded back, with bunches of myrrh and scented aloes exactly where Nicodemus had placed them. The person had left the bed without disturbing the covers, except for a napkin which had been on his face. This was now tidily folded and placed apart.

A step, and John was beside Peter, gazing at the scene with a look of sheer joy on his face. Turning to Peter he whispered, "The Lord is risen!"

Dear Mary, dashing away her tears, stumbling, falling among cruel branches whose leaves thrust into her face, hurried back to the empty tomb and collapsed exhausted in the doorway, her one sobbing thought unanswered – *Where have they laid my Lord? What have they done with him?*

Through her tears as she knelt, she had a blurry vision of two male figures in white sitting at the head and the foot of where Yeshua had lain. Taking her hands from her face, Mary saw that the two were no vision, but real – more real than the room and the empty bedclothes. All gloom and sorrow had fled. Around the visitors was an aura of light and deepest joy. Each was neatly dressed in a white robe to their neck. Their calmness and assurance as they sat, their noble authority and angelic, remote expressions should have comforted Mary in any other situation but this.

"Woman, why are you weeping?" A gentle voice, rich with compassion and heavenly authority.

Hopelessly, Mary replied, between sobs, "Where have they taken my Lord?"

"He is not here," one of them reassured her. "Do you not remember how he explained all these things?"

Mary's tears stopped. She turned and stepped back into the garden. It was so full of life! A tiny waterfall trickled into a pool of shiny pebbles. Rosebuds and more daffodils nodded among the low greenery. Someone else stood near, speaking to her.

"Woman, why are you weeping? Who are you looking for?"

Taking him for the gardener, Mary's tears began again. "O sir, if you have moved him, tell me and I will come and take him away."

The person spoke again – one word. "Mary."

Only one person ever spoke her name like that – he who had restored her soul, drawn her from the muddy pit, rescued her from a wasted life and shown her the healing, everlasting love of God – Yeshua of Nazareth,

The Life of Yeshua

her Master and friend. Now, unbelievably, he stood before her once again, as real as the rock she stood upon.

"Rabboni – my Master!" she cried.

They shared one moment of unutterably joy.

"Do not detain me," Yeshua said. "I have not yet ascended to my Father. Go now and tell my disciples that I shall meet them in Galilee."

As light as air, Mary ran and danced away on her sacred errand.

Chapter Twenty-One

The Feast of Passover was done for another year. Travellers began packing, leading animals and preparing to leave Jerusalem, to pass beneath that great gate and touch the beloved stones for the last time as they passed.

Cleopas and his wife had not far to go, just seven miles to the village of Emmaus. But as they passed beneath the arch, their thoughts were full of confusion. Where had things gone wrong? Yeshua of Nazareth had been invincible. The power of God had been with him and the people clamoured after him. He could have reached out and taken Israel's vacant throne unscathed. The entire nation would have answered his rallying call. The Day of God would have come. Many were ready. Now was the time. Even the Pharisees had said, "There you are, the whole world's gone after him!" What more could he want or ask? What a welcome he'd received! The mile of dusty road leading from Jerusalem's gate was still lined on both sides by fading, wind-blown palm branches. What had gone wrong?

The pair eased into their stride, never long from the subject. People passed them, hurrying in the same direction. Others might join them for a time. Walking with company halved the length of a journey. Someone

The Life of Yeshua

joined them now with a quiet greeting – a stranger evidently – a Galilean by his voice.

"What was that you were talking about? You look so dreadfully sad."

Cleopas stopped. "You mean – you don't know the things which have happened in the City over the past days? You must be a stranger."

"What things?" enquired the man.

"Why – all about Yeshua of Nazareth. He was a great prophet owned of God. His teaching was unanswerable – his power swept aside demons and diseases like chaff in the breeze. It was clear to us that nothing could stop him becoming King of Israel. That was our hope..."

Cleopas shrugged helplessly and re-hoisted his bundle. How could this stranger shed any light on the matter?

The man now did something so impolite that the two travellers were shocked to the core.

"O, foolish people," he said, "so slow to believe all that the prophets taught about Messiah. Did they not tell that the coming Christ must first suffer all these things and then enter into his glory?"

As they continued their walk, the stranger began to open the scriptures from the beginning, reminding them of all the events which pointed towards the Messiah's life, death, his rising again, and his glory. The stranger's explanation lasted the whole seven miles. It was the most exciting display of God's Living Word they had ever experienced, leaving Cleopas and his wife with a warm glow within, and a feeling that they now knew God's plan for the Lord Yeshua better than they knew the route home.

They entered the village of Emmaus with its nestling dwellings. Dusk was falling. The stranger gave a polite wave and would have continued into the darkness, but Cleopas called out, "Sir – do abide with us for a little supper. The day is almost over."

The man responded with some words of thanks and went before his hosts through the open gate. Supper was prepared as Cleopas continued his questions. The stranger's knowledge and love of the Word surpassed even the godliest of the scribes.

They sat at table in the last light of the day, with just one tiny lamp. At a smile from her husband, Mrs Cleopas offered the flat loaf to their visitor. "Would you care to give thanks, dear brother?"

The visitor reached for the loaf, revealing a deep red gash in either hand. With a beautiful prayer, which they recognised instantly, he broke the loaf and handed it to them, and the last light shone upon his dear face. It was their Lord Yeshua, risen indeed and so alive.

As they stared in wonder, the chair at the head of the table was empty, as if it had never been occupied. Husband and wife stared at each other in awe and then at the portions of freshly broken bread in a scattering of crumbs on the table. No words were needed. It was back to Jerusalem to find the disciples. Almost as an afterthought, Cleopas carefully gathered up the broken bread into a bag. Precious hands had held, given thanks and broken that loaf. Silently, he locked the door, joined his wife at the darkened gate and turned his face back towards Jerusalem.

The eleven and their families were all gathered together as the weary couple ascended the stairs and asked to be let in. Shocked, happy faces greeted them, everybody talking at once.

"We've seen the Lord!" Cleopas opened his bag. "He broke the bread – and we knew him!"

The room was filled with joyful, excited voices, but in one moment all sound faded away.

"Shalom, peace to you all!" Yeshua greeted them. He stood near the door which was still barred. He had simply appeared. Then he laughed and moved towards them. "It really is me. I'm not a ghost. Come and see."

He held out his arms. A child timidly touched his hand. He swept her from the floor into the air, and with a cry the company gathered him to themselves.

As if to reassure them, he looked around and said, "Is there any supper?"

The table had not been cleared. They gave him a piece of fish and part of a honeycomb, which he ate before them. Joy arose in their hearts as he then sat down and began to teach – like the old days, but with a wonderful difference.

Now he reminded them that all their treasured scriptures handed down from Moses were all God's gift and plan to guide them to himself – Yeshua. He himself was indeed God's Promised One, who should suffer and die – and then rise to life on the third day. All this had come true. Now, this Good News must be told to the whole world, that Yeshua is the Son of God who died and is alive for evermore – and that all those who turn to God and believe in the Lord Yeshua have that same life, forgiven of all their sins, and a home in Heaven, now and forever. The present disciples were to be the beginning of a great army of messengers who would travel the world and make many other disciples from all nations. And then the Lord Yeshua would return.

The families in that wide room stared at each other in amazement. They – ordinary, simple, uneducated people – were to be the beginning of God's new world family of all those who believe in Yeshua. It would never be easy. Trouble would come, but he would be with them, behind them, within them. How could they understand all this? But here was Yeshua in person – warm, loving, radiating his risen power. They and their children would carry out their task, for he had promised never to leave them. They were to wait right where they were, in Jerusalem, until God should send power for the task ahead.

Someone began to sing a psalm of praise. All joined in until the midnight streets echoed with praise to Israel's great God. Then Yeshua led them in a beautiful prayer.

When they opened their eyes, his place was empty. The door was still barred. His empty dishes lay on the table.

The Life of Yeshua

Judas had gone. Matthias would soon take his place among the twelve. But Thomas had been missing that night. Worried, the others searched for him. They found him buying food in the market. Taking him aside privately they gave him a breathless account of events and took him by the arms.

"Thomas – do you hear? The Lord Yeshua is risen indeed!"

He looked from one to another in disbelief. The events of Thursday and Friday had shattered Thomas completely. Yeshua had been the only friend he had ever really known or trusted. Nothing could harm him, or their friendship. Then suddenly Yeshua was gone. Thomas had stared into a gaping chasm. Still suffering from this, which dealt a severe blow to his faith, he was now being told that the impossible has happened and the whole public deed reversed. It was too much.

He stared back at their radiant faces, then at the quite normal market activity around him. "No," he said firmly, "I cannot – I *will* not – believe unless I can see and touch him for myself, his hands, his side…"

"At least come back," the disciples pleaded. "Remember, the Master chose you to be with us!"

A week later they had gathered together in the upper room. Thomas was with them, gladly welcomed back.

"Strange days," Peter grunted as he dropped the bar across the door to keep out intruders. As he turned, the Master was in the room with them. An awed silence fell.

"Shalom, peace," said the Lord. Some in the room knelt.

Thomas stood frozen, his eyes wide, not in fear but in surprise. The Master moved to face him.

"Thomas," he said, "come. See my hands. Put your hand in my wounded side. It is I. Do not be faithless, but believe!"

Thomas knelt before his Lord in complete recognition and humility. "My Lord and my God!"

Yeshua said to him, "Thomas, because you have seen me, you now believe. How blessed are those who believe yet have never seen me."

They were indeed strange and wonderful days. Whatever was to happen next, Jerusalem still held the answer.

Nathaniel of Cana had some business in Galilee. Leaving five of their number at the upper room, he, with Peter and a few others, set off. Nathaniel's business completed, they wandered along the seashore in the cool of the evening. They walked upon wave-lapped stones of Tabga beach as the crescent moon arose, sparkling among the wave-tops. Peter's larger boat was there, its stern supported each side by a beam of timber. Perhaps they might sleep on board? *Exciting prospect!* Peter had a better idea. His eyes shone with challenge.

"Well lads – I'm going fishing!"

An enthusiastic cheer echoed his words. "And we'll all come with you!"

Willing hands steadied the vessel and heaved her into the foam. A splashing of feet, a scramble and all were on board, happy to be occupied, days of tension crowned with adventure. None was happier than Captain Peter, back in his old trade, using his energies to shake out the nets, let down the sail and attend to the steering. The crew would have burst into song had it not been for the golden rule.

The boat glided out beneath the stars until no land was visible – the slightest breeze, a flat calm – ideal conditions. After leaving brief instructions, Peter stripped off his top, took the pole of the net, and slid over the side, swimming away with powerful strokes. At maximum length he trod water and began to curve the heavy net back towards the ship. *Such a night!* Something was bound to happen.

But nothing did. Peter repeated the operation until even he was exhausted.

With water still glistening on his chest, he showed the non-professional members of the crew how to bundle and hurl the other net high in the air, unfolding as it fell splashing into the water. Careful fishers could do this with the minimum of disturbance.

The hours passed slowly. Enthusiasm waned, first among the landsmen, until, at last, as pink dawn touched the horizon, even Peter, fisherman supreme, had to admit defeat.

All was shipshape. There were no jobs the amateur crew could busy themselves with to hide their disappointment. Their vision of a fishless breakfast on the beach, warming their hands around a tiny fire, was not an inviting prospect. No one blamed Peter. It had been a good idea, but a few fish would have crowned the moment and set them all singing.

The daylight grew. Not far now.

"Look!" someone said. A man was walking along the beach, near the water's edge.

He seemed to know Peter's aiming point, despite the absence of a row of empty, waiting pots. As the boat drew nearer he called out, faint but clear, "Any catch, lads?"

He must be an early morning customer. All eyes were upon him as Peter cupped his hands and replied, "Nothing at all tonight – sorry!"

Instead of waving and moving off, the distant stranger stayed. He made a wide gesture. "Cast your net on the right side of the ship and you will find."

Weary arms enfolded the heap of soaking net once more and almost mechanically hurled the unwinding mass as high as their fading strength would allow. It came down with an uneven splatter and sank instantly, the worst cast of the night.

At once something happened. With a scream the guide ropes tightened, dragging the vessel to a halt. The crew ran to the stern, as a huge silvery globe swung into view in the deep water, defying all attempts to slacken the ropes and draw it to the surface.

While the five watched from the stern, John remained in the prow unable to take his eyes from the figure on the beach a hundred yards away. Peter joined him. John said, "It is the Lord!"

Instantly, Peter struggled into his coat and without a word dropped into the sea, swimming towards the beach where the Lord Yeshua stood.

It took the crew's combined effort, without Peter, to beach the ship and draw up the living, thrashing catch, straining the net to bursting point – but not beyond! It was clearly a great miracle!

A beautiful fire flamed and crackled within a circle of stones. Upon these lay freshly-turned fish, almost ready. Fresh bread lay in two piles on a clean cloth. The damp disciples hesitated, the fire glowing on their faces.

The Lord held out his arms. "Come and have breakfast. Bring some of the fish you caught."

With a monumental effort Peter dragged the net on to the dry stones and released the draw-cord. Huge, edible fish slithered out all around him (later they counted one hundred and fifty three), each one a feast in itself. Peter carried three and set them as they were upon the hot stones. The disciples gasped in surprise at their size and richness, glancing in awe at the Master busily serving smoking fish with broken bread, as if the dramas of the past few days had never happened. They ate hungrily but as if in a dream.

Scriptures began to take on new meaning.

"He opens his hand and every living thing is fed."

"See if I will not open the windows of Heaven and pour out for you such a blessing that you will not have room to receive it."

"I will never leave you, never forsake you."

Chapter Twenty-Two

Together again, the Twelve met constantly in that same upstairs room as the Master had instructed. They met as families, eating together, the Twelve learning to pray as the Master had taught them. Patiently they waited for the Promise from Heaven which would enable them, as ordinary people, to go into the whole world and tell people of all nations God's message of forgiveness and eternal life through believing in his Son, Yeshua, and how God had sealed this offer of forgiveness by raising Yeshua alive from the dead.

Some of the words which Yeshua had spoken to them were also becoming clear to them.

"I and my Father are one."

"You have believed in God, now also believe in me."

"Without me you can do nothing."

"No one who comes to me shall ever be sent away."

John, when he began to grow old wrote, "The Lord Yeshua did many other signs which are not written in this book (the Gospel of John). These are chosen to help you believe that Yeshua truly is the Son of God, and that in believing, you may have life in his name."

*You will show me the path of life.
In your presence is fullness of joy.
At your right hand are pleasures for evermore.*

Psalm 16, verse 11

Also from the Publisher

It's Me: Jesus
David J. Aston

The four gospels retold as JESUS might have told the story himself.
Join Jesus on a journey of friendship, laughter, revelation and hardships. Following him on the donkey into Jerusalem. Listening as he talks about the creation. Watching as he restores people to health and wholeness. Accompanying him on the hard road to the cross.

My Son, the Messiah
Raymond Smith

Throughout the whole Roman Empire it was what every mother dreaded: crouching at the foot of a wooden stake, waiting for your son to breathe his last and to bring an end to hours of excruciating pain and torture.
As well as the usual feelings that somehow it was wrong that the child should die before his mother, there was the confusion as to why my son, my firstborn, should be in that awful situation. Why was he being treated as a criminal? And not just any criminal, but on a par with insurrectionists?

Available from **www.onwardsandupwards.org**